JOAN DALTON

MARILYN WATSON

Among Friends

Classrooms Where Caring and Learning Prevail

DEVELOPMENTAL STUDIES CENTER

Funding to support the development, piloting, and dissemination of Developmental Studies Center programs has been provided by the following:

The Annenberg Foundation, Inc.

Anonymous Donor

Center for Substance Abuse Prevention, Substance Abuse and Mental Health Services Agency, U.S. Department of Health and Human Services

The Danforth Foundation

The Ford Foundation

Evelyn and Walter Haas, Jr. Fund

Clarence E. Heller Charitable Foundation

The William and Flora Hewlett Foundation

The Robert Wood Johnson Foundation

The Walter S. Johnson Foundation

Ewing Marion Kauffman Foundation

W.K. Kellogg Foundation

John S. and James L. Knight Foundation

Lilly Endowment, Inc.

The John D. and Catherine T. MacArthur Foundation

A.L. Mailman Family Foundation, Inc.

Charles Stewart Mott Foundation

National Institute on Drug Abuse

National Science Foundation

Nippon Life Insurance Foundation

The Pew Charitable Trusts

The Rockefeller Foundation

Louise and Claude Rosenberg, Jr.

The San Francisco Foundation

Shinnyo-En Foundation

The Spencer Foundation

Spunk Fund, Inc.

Stuart Foundations

Surdna Foundation, Inc.

DeWitt Wallace–Reader's Digest Fund, Inc.

Wells Fargo Bank

To the wonderful teachers who made this book possible

— JOAN AND MARILYN

To John

*who has always provided the right balance
of challenge and support*

— MARILYN

CONTENTS

PREFACE

O UR COLLABORATION began several years ago, on two different continents, where we each were engaged with some very similar objectives about learning and teaching: Joan, as a widely respected teacher and educator in Australia, known especially for her extensive work in the field of cooperative learning; and Marilyn, as the program director of the Child Development Project (CDP), a research-based initiative helping schools across the United Stated to develop caring learning communities. Our educational philosophies were highly compatible—so compatible that CDP invited Joan to be the keynote speaker at one of its professional development institutes; her stories about the wonderful ways that Australian teachers were working with children proved very inspirational to the teachers and CDP staff at the institute. A year later, when Marilyn began planning a book intended to capture not only the theory and principles of CDP but also relevant stories of real teachers and children, she asked Joan to join her.

In its work with teachers, CDP has provided classroom materials and guiding principles based on current theory and research, but it is the teachers who find ways to bring these principles to life in their classrooms. In writing this book, we have set out to capture in explicit and concrete ways the wisdom of a few of these teachers and to make their wisdom

Dawn Biscardi
I try to plant the seeds that we're not learning in little boxes, we're learning together.
Grade 3
George Washington School
White Plains, New York

Cindy Brooks
It doesn't matter whether children are in kinder-garten or sixth grade, they need to build trust if you want to develop a coopera-tive classroom.
Grade 5–6
Louis E. Stocklmeir School
Sunnyvale, California

Nancy Day Chapel
Children feel that they are a part of the classroom and feel good about themselves, so learning is more fun.
Grade 1
Sedgwick School
Cupertino, California

Deborah Claypool
I try to let children know
I'm a real person.
Grade 1
Hazelwood Elementary
School, Louisville, Kentucky

Laurel Cress
I am concerned with what
the kids think and what is
important to them—it is
part of respecting them.
And it is a big part of how a
caring community happens.
Grade 3 Bilingual
Longwood School
Hayward, California

Marcia Davis
Beyond helping kids see
what they have in common,
we also do things that help
kids recognize and value
their individuality.
Grade 2–3
Hazelwood Elementary
School, Louisville, Kentucky

available to others. The teachers who form the heart of this book opened their classrooms to us and spent many hours talking with us; we have incorporated these visits and conversations to bring you, the reader, into their classrooms and to give you a chance to hear their thinking, struggles, and triumphs.

These teachers have different teaching styles, teach at different grade levels, have different student populations, and work in a wide range of settings—yet there are strong commonalties across their classrooms. Each of them, in his or her own way, focuses on building kind and respectful relationships with and among students. Each is explicit about teaching humane values. Each draws upon students' internal motivation to learn and to contribute. And each teaches in ways that support students' active construction of knowledge. As you will see in the chapters that follow, these teachers understand and capitalize on what we call the "four keys to classroom community."

Writing this book was a joint effort, and although our contributions to the manuscript have been different, they have been equally important to the overall structure and content of the book. While both of us have talked with and visited the classrooms of all of these teachers, Joan captured in writing their conversations, their reflections, and the realities of their classrooms. Both of us have contributed to the overall theoretical perspective that guided the creation of this book, but Marilyn is primarily responsible for the theoretical principles that form the basis of CDP and frame the activities and conversations found in these pages. We, like the teachers whom you will meet, have different voices or writing styles; this book was edited to blend our authorial voices as well as to fit with the style and tone of other books published by Developmental Studies Center (CDP's parent agency).

ACKNOWLEDGMENTS

There are many people to thank for making this book possible. In addition to the class-room teachers whose contributions are specifically featured in the book, we wish to thank the literally hundreds of teachers, principals, and staff developers in the schools and districts where CDP has been implemented and honed to its current form. CDP and this book have greatly benefited from their insights, challenges, and suggestions.

The research staff of CDP—notably Dan Solomon, Vic Battistich, and Catherine Lewis—have not only provided data to help evaluate CDP and understand the effects of caring communities on students, but they have also contributed importantly to the ideas inherent in CDP and this book. Likewise, we owe tremendous thanks to the program staff of CDP, especially Sylvia Kendzior, Stefan Dasho, Colombe Allen, Fran Chamberlain, Pat Eppard, Gil Guillermo, Awele Makeba, and Dorothy Steele; they not only contributed to our ideas, but they also worked with the teachers and principals to help make CDP a reality—not just a set of ideas. And finally, many conversations over the years with Eric Schaps, president of the Developmental Studies Center and director of the Child Development Project, have greatly shaped the nature of CDP and of our thinking. We wish to thank all these people for helping to make this book better than it might otherwise have been; they are not, however, responsible for any errors or confusions that remain.

Lynn Murphy edited this book with great care, contributing not only to its style and clari-ty, but also to its substance. Anne Goddard and Alice Klein provided thoughtful copyedit-ing. Photographs and some vignettes were taken from videotapes produced by Peter Shwartz; additional photographs were contributed by Jim Ketsdever. Allan Ferguson designed the book and made the page layouts inviting and clear, and Visual Strategies designed the cover.

Joan Dalton
Marilyn Watson

INTRODUCTION

ALL OF US are more comfortable among friends. We are more willing to take risks, say what we think, and ask about what we don't understand. We know our friends will provide help and support when we need it and continue to think well of us even through the rough spots. The same is true for children in school—it's important to be among friends. As early as kindergarten, having a friend is a predictor of children's long-term success in school.

In a Friendly Place

When children feel that their classrooms are friendly places—that their teachers and classmates care about them and that their ideas and concerns have importance—those children

- trust and respect their teachers more,
- like school more,
- enjoy challenging learning activities more,
- are concerned about others and more willing to help, and
- are better able to resolve conflicts fairly and without force.

In short, when children feel that they are among friends in their schools and classrooms, they make the school community their own. And in committing to the school community's values, they become more engaged in learning and more thoughtful and caring in their behavior.

Friendly classrooms don't just happen, of course. They take considerable effort on the part of both teachers and students—more deliberate effort than may have been required in the past. But increasingly, this new emphasis on building community is being recognized as valid and important. As the world changes, as children's environment changes, the profession of teaching responds.

In a Changing World

We all recognize that our classes are becoming more diverse and that more and more students have backgrounds and experiences different from ours and different from one another's'. Correspondingly, as teachers we have begun devoting more time to understanding and valuing those differences—and to helping children understand and value one another. In addition, as other adults in children's lives have less time to spend with them and as neighborhoods operate less as communities where people know and help one another, we as teachers have begun to more deliberately provide children with the experience of membership in a community—their school and classroom community—and more focused in helping them acquire the skills for maintaining community.

We may not have been trained to do this; we may have entered the teaching profession at a time when classrooms were more homogeneous, children went to the same school with the same people year after year, and neighborhoods were extensions of family. But the world

Laura Ecken
It dawned on me gradually that this way of working with kids is a philosophy that permeates your whole way of teaching and living, even your way of dealing with your family.
Grade 2–3
Hazelwood Elementary
School, Louisville, Kentucky

Laura Havis
Kids are learning to set high standards for themselves.
Grade 3
Ridgeway School
White Plains, New York

Brenda Henderson
I always wanted to jump in and solve all of the children's problems. But then I began to realize this was not in their best interests.
Grade 4 AP
Auburndale Elementary
School, Louisville, Kentucky

Carole Lewis
Change takes a lot of energy, but I have reshaped my classroom practice. It feels like "our" classroom, and I could never go back to having it be just "my" classroom.
Grade 5–6
Sedgwick School
Cupertino, California

Louise Lotz
Over the year I sit in the seats of all my children and try to think about how they see the world.
Grade 1
Bollinger Canyon Elementary School
San Ramon, California

Karla Moore
I am trying to help children build meaning, rather than just me telling them.
Grade 1
Laurel Wood School
Salinas, California

changes. Precisely because fewer of our students have had rich community experiences, we must focus more than ever on teaching the basic values and skills of community membership—the importance of kindness, respect, and personal responsibility; how to be a friend; how not to hurt others' feelings; how to settle disagreements fairly, compromise, apologize, and make reparations for harm done; how to communicate feelings and show respect; how to help one another and ask for help. And, as we are well aware, this is all the more difficult given the contrary lessons children see daily on their television screens if not on their streets—being cool rather than kind, getting away with things rather than taking responsibility, manipulating others to your own advantage, demonstrating wit with sarcastic put-downs.

And so, on the cusp of the twenty-first century, children encounter a world that has become more complex, diverse, and impersonal than ever before. No longer do they grow up and remain in an environment of monolithic adult values and watchfulness; nor do they interact exclusively within a web of personal relationships and loyalties. In the absence of these experiences, children need more than ever to understand the reasons for humane values and how to practice them of their own free will. There is no amount of surveillance, for example, that can prevent the thousands of opportunities each of them will have to take unfair advantage, despoil the environment, or treat unkindly those who cannot protect themselves. In a world where children are increasingly on their own, it has never been more important for us, in our role as teachers, to foster our students' deep understanding of and internal commitment to the values that will keep us all humane.

In addition to the changes in our social institutions, changes in the workplace are causing us to change the way we teach. For several decades educators have paid lip service to evolving workplace needs, but only recently have we begun to actually change what and how we teach to meet those needs. Instead of continuing to prepare students for the solitary and repetitive jobs of assembly lines and typing pools, we are increasingly teaching in ways that prepare students for jobs in which they must work collaboratively with others, exercise judgment, apply complex and diverse bodies of knowledge, continue to learn, and generate creative solutions to problems. We have always provided such an education for some students; today we must find ways to provide such an education for all students. The assembly line, like the neighborhood grocer, has changed, if not disappeared.

We know our job as teachers has become more complex and demanding: we find ourselves charged with creating classroom communities where all children feel valued and cared for,

Lizbeth Nastari
All of the community building we did made for
a very safe classroom.
Grade 4
Louis E. Stocklmeir School
Sunnyvale, California

Becky O'Bryan
I am no longer the person on center stage. I have learned to trust the kids.
Grade 4–5 AP
Auburndale Elementary School, Louisville, Kentucky

Terry Rice
Our classroom learning has a social focus as well as an academic one.
Grade 6
Longwood School
Hayward, California

Maria Vallejo
If there is a problem, I ask
"What is the problem? How
can you solve it?"
Kindergarten
El Gabilan School
Salinas, California

Fran Zimmerman
Partners are very important
for young children.
Grade 1
Ridgeway School
White Plains, New York

and where all children learn at deeper levels than they ever have in the past. No matter how we have been trained to teach, no matter what we have been prepared to expect, the struggle to create such powerful learning communities has engaged us all.

In this book we share with you some of the ways that we and others have found to create such communities—classrooms where every child feels among friends, where caring and learning prevail.

Four Keys to Classroom Community

FOSTERING CARING RELATIONSHIPS

TEACHING HUMANE VALUES

HONORING INTRINSIC MOTIVATION

LEARNING FOR UNDERSTANDING

Fostering Caring Relationships

WHEN WE UNDERSTAND THAT building caring classroom relationships is the key to creating a successful learning community, we naturally design the first weeks of school to help everyone feel comfortable and learn about each other—and we integrate these opportunities into our academic programs and into the life of the classroom throughout the year. As teacher Nancy Day Chapel points out, "Learning is more fun because children feel that they are a part of the classroom and they feel good about themselves."

Beginning the Year with Care

IN THE FOLLOWING classroom visits and collegial conversations, we see the strategic importance of starting the year with care—planning and taking time for children to become comfortable and feel included in the classroom community.

 **You Gotta Shut Up**

No amount of planning for children's first experiences together can anticipate every possible friction, but even despite such rough spots, the brief encounter below demonstrates how instinctive it is for children to want to feel connected with each other.

> It was the first week of school. Stephen and Mike, two seven-year-olds, were assigned to work together on an academic task. Stephen sat down beside some classroom shelves and began playing with the materials on the shelves, pointedly not looking at Mike.

MIKE   What's wrong?

STEPHEN   *(Without looking at Mike)* I don't feel good.

MIKE   We gotta write about . . .

STEPHEN   *(Still without looking at Mike)* You gotta shut up!

MIKE   *(Leaning toward Stephen inquisitively)* Unless you do not want to be my partner?

STEPHEN   *(Ignoring the question and turning to Mike)* You got a bike?

MIKE   *(Nods)*

STEPHEN   Well, then, I might come over.

MIKE   My house is red and it has two trees in the front of it.

STEPHEN   What's your name?

MIKE   Mike.

STEPHEN   Are we supposed to write something?

SOME POINTS TO CONSIDER

✔ There may well be several reasons why Stephen had difficulty starting his work with Mike, but it is hard not to sense a little boy trying in his way to control a situation that felt arbitrary and unsafe—Stephen did not even know Mike's name. Once he found a way to connect with Mike—in this case, by establishing that Mike was a person who had a bicycle—he felt ready to get to work.

✔ Just as this scene highlights how important it is for children (and not *just* children) to feel personal connections in order to work effectively with others, it also demonstrates that relationships, which are at the heart of a collaborative community of learners, begin from the very first moments of the school year.

 Have a Nice Weekend, Brett

For most children, the insecurities that come with the first days of school are inevitable. As Louise Lotz has found, however, her first-graders respond to a little personal attention and knowing exactly what is expected of them.

> It was Friday afternoon, the end of the first week of school. Louise gathered her students together in a circle.

> LOUISE   This is our first Friday together, and every Friday we are going to get together and talk about our week. Who remembers one thing we did together?

> MITCHELL   We drew stuff about helping.

> JAMES   We talked about ways we come to school.

> MARY   P.E.

> ELLIE   We did pictures . . . and we learned how to get our own space.

> SAM   We learned how to get water.

> MITCHELL   We went around the school.

> Louise acknowledged each contribution with an encouraging smile, nod, or brief comment. She then scanned the circle, waiting for any further contributions.

LOUISE I want everybody to stop and think in your head about an activity you have enjoyed this week. I will share mine: the activity I enjoyed most this week was reading to you books that I love.

    Victor, can you tell us your favorite activity this week?

VICTOR *(Looking shyly at Louise and not answering)*

LOUISE *(Modeling further)* You could say "My favorite activity was . . ." or "The thing I enjoyed most this week . . ."

VICTOR *(Looking even shyer)*

LOUISE That's okay. We can come back to your turn later if you think of something you would like to share. Who else has a favorite activity?

KERRY When you took our pictures.

    (As the children go around the circle, one child begins whistling loudly)

LOUISE Oh, I hear an outside noise. *(She waits and the whistling stops)*

As sharing continued, Louise courteously acknowledged each contribution and remembered to come back to Daniel, who had said he was "still thinking." She did not pressure anyone to comment, and she honored the fact that two or three children decline to speak; what was important was that everybody had the opportunity to contribute.

LOUISE Well, we have had quite a week, and now we need to get ready to go home.

As children left the circle, four at a time by table groups, Victor finally realized *who* was the highlight of his week—and he gave Louise a quick hug!

At their tables, children watched as Louise helped one table group model the Friday afternoon ritual of stacking their chairs for the weekend room cleaning. "When your chairs are stacked up," she concluded, "you may line up."

As the children left the room, Louise's individual good-byes—"Good-bye, Lauren. I hope you enjoy visiting your friend," "Have a nice weekend, Brett"—mingled with their happy responses. The several hugs that Louise received said much about the relationships that were forming and suggested that the children had indeed enjoyed their first week in first grade.

Jim Ketsdever

In Louise Lotz's first grade, children learn from the very first day of school that their teacher is a member of the classroom community as well as its leader.

SOME POINTS TO CONSIDER

✔ This seemingly simple scenario demonstrates several essential elements of laying the foundations of a collaborative classroom community. Louise is spending time during these first days establishing what is valued in such a community—as Mitchell's comment, "We drew stuff about helping," reflects. Most significantly, children learn that they are valued and that their voices are valued. Louise designs the first-week activities to connect to her students' personal lives—to help them get to know each other, to be enjoyable, and to help them form the trusting relationships that will allow them to work together effectively.

✔ Louise's manner with children also reflects her commitment to this relationship building. She encourages and guides children in a caring and authoritative way, and she models her own membership in the community by sharing what she has enjoyed most during the week.

✔ The scene also shows how hard Louise works to familiarize children with routines, procedures, and expectations so that they feel secure and understand what is wanted of them. The time and modeling it takes to establish routines—for example, stacking chairs and lining up to leave for the day—are small but important pieces that contribute to a smoothly functioning classroom. Indeed, children's comments—"We learned how to get water," "We learned how to get our own space"—reflect how important it is to them to feel familiar with such routines.

 I Did Not Sleep the Night before School Began

Louise is an experienced teacher who understands that the relationships and expectations that are established during the first weeks of school are critical to what happens throughout the rest of the year. She takes time to build the supportive environment children need to be successful learners and members of the community. In the interview below, Joan asked her to describe some of the planning that goes into the first day of school.

JOAN   Would you describe how you prepare for the first day of school?

LOUISE   I did not sleep the night before school began. Mainly, I thought about making sure each child would feel comfortable, that I would get each child off to a good start. I wanted to be sure I reached each child.

The day before school I got the student profile cards from the teachers my students had last year, read through them carefully, and thought about children's seating arrangements. Then I asked those teachers to come in and see whether the way I had placed the name tags on tables was okay—whether there were any potential problems with the table groupings I had done.

I sat in the seats of the children who seemed to have had a difficult time last year in kindergarten, and I thought about them and how I could make it a good year for them. I do this at particular times with all of my children over the year, and I try to think about how they see the world—their perspective on things.

JOAN   What did children see that first morning as they walked into your room?

LOUISE   That morning I had the door wide open so that children could come in early with their parents. I had a big welcome sign on the door that also described how parents could help children put their belongings away and explore the room.

I walked around and greeted everybody, and when everyone had arrived I asked children to come and sit on the carpet with me. I welcomed the children and told them a little bit about myself. When I called roll I explained that every day when I do this I like to say "good morning" to each of them. Then we went outside and one of the parents took a class picture.

JOAN   Lead us through the rest of the day. What other community-building things did you do?

LOUISE   During the day we read some favorite books—for example, *Where Does the Teacher Live?*—and I told children about me when I was in first grade and how my teacher lived around the corner. We went on a school tour, and then children talked in table groups about the different ways they come to school. We made a class graph to show whether they come by car, bicycle, or walking.

From the responses of some children, it was obvious that they saw the graphing as a competition and that they wanted to be in the graph category that had the most people. Some even talked about winning and losing!

JOAN   How did you refocus children on building community instead of competing?

LOUISE   I explained that we were collecting the graph information so that children who walked to school could walk together, so that we would know who came by car in case someone needed a ride, and so on.

After that, we introduced our September calendar and children drew pictures of "Here I am on the first day of school." We finished in a circle, with children showing their pictures and sharing what they liked about the first day of school.

JOAN   You seem to like giving children opportunities to talk to the group, even if they just go around the circle and make simple statements.

LOUISE   Yes—to my mind, having children hear each other is at least as powerful a way to build community as doing special community-building activities.

A POINT TO CONSIDER

✔ Over the course of her teaching career, Louise has learned how to plan the first day of school so that students feel they are entering a caring community. She has also learned—and it keeps her awake sometimes—how to recognize each child as a distinctive person with unique needs, experiences, and perspective. Perhaps this recognition is what leads Louise so naturally to focus on building a classroom community: When everyone counts, everyone can contribute; when everyone can contribute, everyone can learn.

You Want Them to Go Home Eager to Return

Regardless of the ages of their students, consistent themes emerge in conversations with teachers who, like Louise, deliberately plan their first days of school to build a sense of community. In the following collegial conversation, Joan interviewed teachers Deborah Claypool, Laura Ecken, Marcia Davis, Brenda Henderson, and Becky O'Bryan—whose classrooms range from grade one through five.

JOAN   What are some of the things you do to build a feeling of community right from the first day of school?

DEBORAH   Children do a lot of personal sharing in our classroom, and as the teacher, I do a lot of sharing and telling about myself. When I think back on what really frightened me when I was in grade school, for the most part it was my teachers. So I try to let children know I'm a real person. For example, I let them know that, like some of them, I'm nervous when school is beginning. And I bring in things that are important to me—objects and photographs that I share with them.

But first of all, these are first-graders, so I focus on reassuring them. Within the first hour of the first day I make sure I tell them: "I'm going to show you where the restrooms are," "I'm going to take you to lunch," "I'm going to show you how to pay your money." Then we can start to work on getting comfortable as a group.

BECKY   Even fifth-graders have those same kinds of concerns. We spend the last hour of the first day just talking: "What questions do you have?" "What concerns do you have?" "What are you nervous about?" And you know, their questions are things like, "When are we going to get lockers?" and "Will we have snack time?" Those things that may not be important to us are important to those kids sitting there!

LAURA   One of the things I do on that first day—before children really size each other up too much and decide, "That person isn't someone I would be friends with"—is an activity that gets us all moving around the room and talking to a lot of different people to find out what we have in common. I give the class questions that I know a lot of kids are going to have the same answers to, like, "What is your favorite TV show?" It's real helpful because they find out right away, "Hey, these people are like me!"

MARCIA   Beyond helping kids see what they have in common, we also do things that help kids recognize and value their individuality. We graph all the data we gather—about birthdays and siblings and so forth—and end up with charts all over the place that help us see who we are as individuals *and* as a community.

BECKY   We use a lot of writing about ourselves as a way of getting to know each other. The first day of school, I write and copy for each of them a letter telling about me and my family. And I ask them to write a letter back. I also write a letter to the parents and ask them to write back and give me some input about their child.

BRENDA   We use writing, too. I had several children who were new to the school this year, and that was difficult because a lot of children in my class have been at Auburndale for five years and so are really comfortable with each other. So children wrote letters to the new students telling them all sorts of things they thought it would be useful for them to know. We also sang songs to the new students and they took home a card from all of us to welcome them and give them a sense of belonging to the group.

JOAN   Beyond what you actually do *on* the first day of school, what goes through your mind when you are anticipating and planning for it?

LAURA   There's a lot of pressure around that first day because things have to go smoothly, be interesting to the kids, and not get them into situations where you have to be correcting them—you want everybody to feel really welcome. I spend a lot of time planning how everything will go. You want it to be just a comfortable, friendly, happy time for kids.

BECKY   I agree with Laura about that first-day pressure. And I have to remind myself on that first day that these are *not* the same group of kids I had last May. I have to keep saying to myself, "Slow down, Becky, slow down. Talk, model, explain. Don't worry about getting through everything. Follow the kids' lead. If they need a little more time to talk about something, let it go. Just watch them—during snack time, free time—just watch, you can learn so much!"

          At the end of that first day of school, you want children to go home eager to return, to go home feeling that they have a place in that class, a place where they belong, a place where they're secure and comfortable—a place where they can be confident. I try to plan first-day activities so that everyone can be successful and have the opportunity to share with each other. I want every child to have made contact with at least one other child that they can go home feeling good about. And I want them to be able to go home feeling they have a personal connection with me—to be able to report, "Mrs. O'Bryan said this or that to me."

✔ These teachers voice what all teachers want for their students—for them to feel secure and confident, to be happy and successful—and their comments reflect the careful thinking and planning necessary to achieve these goals. From the first day of the school year, these teachers focus on building relationships—teacher-child, child-teacher, and child-child.

✔ They plan simple but engaging activities through which children and teacher can get to know each other and learn something about each other's lives outside the classroom—activities that acknowledge individuality and difference and at the same time promote community and a sense of belonging to the group.

✔ They recognize that children's questions and concerns may be different from those they think of as teachers; they put themselves in the place of their students, take their students' perspective, and try to learn from them.

Helping Children Get to Know Each Other

Helping children get to know each other is not just a "nice" thing to do, or something that's over after the first day of school, or even optional. The teachers in this book say that helping children get to know each other is essential, and they have a lot of practical suggestions for how to do so.

 There Was a Big Piece Missing

Whether they have always focused on helping their students get to know each other or have just recently begun making time for it, teachers Marcia Davis, Laura Ecken, Lizbeth Nastari, and Nancy Day Chapel agreed that building a friendly culture is well worth the time it takes.

MARCIA If I'm a child, I'm not going to share in a group if I don't feel comfortable—safe and accepted. If I don't know and trust the other kids in my group, I'm not going to have the confidence to contribute. I'm not going to be sure how my ideas will be accepted.

LAURA   And I'm not going to be able to share if I haven't had any practice in learning how to do that. You can't throw kids together in a group and expect them to work out the dynamics of what goes on in a group *and* do an academically challenging activity at the same time. First they need time to get to know each other in non-threatening ways, and they need some practice with group dynamics. They have to do that first.

NANCY   I used to expect that children would come into class at the beginning of the year and open their books and get to work. I was very academics-oriented. But there was a big piece missing—I wasn't taking time to have children get to know each other, I wasn't taking time to build community.

Now that I'm taking the time to do this, I'm realizing that my students really needed these steps all along—to be able to get the academics. I see them showing more positive attitudes toward learning—learning is more fun because children feel that they are a part of the classroom and they feel good about themselves. They have this harmony within themselves and it is helping their academic learning.

LIZBETH   I'm conscious of the need to get academic things going, but in looking back at last year's lesson plans, I realized that all of the community building we did first made for a very safe classroom. I really enjoyed last year. The community building we did meant a lot to me and I was a better teacher for it. And I'm sure the children learned more in the long run because of it.

SOME POINTS TO CONSIDER

✔ These teachers take time early to help students get comfortable working together—and they reap the benefits throughout the year. They find that giving students many small-group experiences in low-pressure, high-interest activities helps group members discover they can enjoy and trust each other.

✔ They understand that groups don't automatically know how to work together. They take time for "practice" activities that have the explicit purpose of getting children accustomed to working together.

✔ They also find that giving children time to become comfortable with each other before introducing academically demanding group work results in stronger academic performances throughout the rest of the school year.

Learning Activities that Support a Friendly Culture

W HILE THE teachers in this book recognize the crucial importance of community-building activities, these are just one strategy in their effort to build a friendly culture in their classrooms. Overall, it is the content of their curriculum *and* their approach to classroom management that create a classroom environment in which everyone counts and everyone contributes.

 **Friendly Evidence**

Laura Ecken and Marcia Davis, who each teach a multiage grade two-three class, coplanned their curriculum for the start of year around the theme of "friendship." This theme obviously was chosen to signal an important value in their classrooms; likewise, the variety of group work, partner work, and whole-class sharing that the students experienced while working on the curriculum signaled another important value: that there are many ways to contribute.

> By the second week of school, Marcia's and Laura's walls were covered with student work that visually reinforced the consistent message about what their classroom communities valued.

- Poems by small groups describe things classmates can do together as friends.

- Children's drawings show things they can do with a friend. Brandon captioned his picture, "I can play frisbee with a friend."

- Partners' Venn diagrams show "Ways We Are Alike" and "Ways We Are Different."

- Children's captioned paintings let them tell the class something special about themselves. Marshelle's painting demonstrates her pleasure that "I can check the mailbox."

- "Our Friendly Class" bulletin board displays each class member's cutout self-portrait—including the teacher's, of course.

- Students contribute their ideas to class posters about such topics as "Favorite Books," "What Would You Like to Learn This Year?" and "Weekend Plans with My Family."

- A daily chalkboard note greets everyone: "Welcome class! Today is Monday, September 13. We go to P.E. today for the first time. I know you are excited. We will read *Miss Maggie* again. Remember her friendship with Nat? We will pretend to be Miss Maggie and Nat. Have a great day!"

- A class mindmap suggests conversation topics for "friendly lunchtime chats."

- A bulletin board displays partners' drawings about "Our Lunch Buddies." Jessica's and Erica's each show the other chomping on a favorite food, captioned "I learned that Erica likes hamburger" and "I learned that Jessica likes to eat pizza."

- A class book and photo album features a picture of each child (and the teacher), along with salient information supplied by a partner. Traci wrote, "Shirley likes to ride her bike. She has 3 brothers."

As is evident from the activities Marcia's and Laura's students experienced, partner interviews are a mainstay of building a classroom community, and they also promote all kinds of communication and thinking skills—questioning, relating, listening, visualizing, summarizing, writing, and drawing.

A variety of other community-building activities are described on pages 175–177 in the Resources section of this book. Such activities are valuable not only at the beginning of the year, but also to facilitate many events and transitions in classroom life: to reacquaint students after long vacations; when new students enter the class; before small groups embark on a complex project; when students are moving from working with partners to working with larger groups; and when new groups are forming.

 You Brought It in a Bag and Kept It a Secret

Partner interviews are such a rich structure for integrating academics and a friendly culture that it is worth observing one in some detail. The following interview activity, which was captured on videotape* in Laurel Cress's third-grade classroom several weeks into the school year, shows how much children learn from their teacher's modeling and from their own interactions.

As Laurel and her aide, Anna Ramirez, settled into small chairs beside each other, students arranged themselves on the carpet in front of them.

* Excerpted from DSC Video Library, "Talking Artifacts."

LAUREL   Today we are going to do another partner interview like some you have done in the past. Even last week we did one—remember? When you switched desks and interviewed your new desk partner to find out how they were like you and how they were different from you?

This interview will be a little different, though. Today you brought in artifacts—special things that are special to you from home—and you brought them in a bag and kept them a secret.

Children smiled at the thought of their "secrets" and were clearly eager to have a chance to show them. Laurel returned their smiles and continued.

LAUREL   You will interview a partner to find out what they brought. Mrs. Ramirez and I are going to show you what you will be doing with your partner, and we will be doing it like a little play. So . . . you are the audience, and I am going to give you a job to do. I want you to listen to us and look for how we are being good listeners for each other, and look for what we are doing to find out more information about the other person's story. We're going to talk about this afterwards.

Laurel and Mrs. Ramirez turned their chairs so that they were facing each other. Removing a photo from her paper bag, Laurel began.

LAUREL   My special thing is a picture of my best friend from first grade right through fourth grade, when I was in elementary school. She gave this picture to me on Valentine's Day in fourth grade, and that was also the day she moved away. I remember that day. I remember playing in the boxes that were waiting for the moving van, and I can remember waving good-bye to her. I can even remember what I did after she left. I was feeling kind of strange and I went and played a Mary Poppins record and colored and I was thinking of my friend.

Children sat quietly, engrossed in Laurel's special memories of her friend. Mrs. Ramirez also was caught up in Laurel's story, but then remembered her role as the interviewer.

MRS.
RAMIREZ   What is her name?

LAUREL   Oh, her name is Eve.

MRS.
RAMIREZ   Where does she live now?

LAUREL	That day she moved to Hawaii, but then she got married to a man who lived in Canada, so now she lives in Canada.
MRS. RAMIREZ	Have you seen her since?

Laurel described the times she has seen her friend since and told about the most recent time, when she went to her friend's wedding in Canada.

MRS. RAMIREZ	What was your favorite thing to do when you were together?
LAUREL	Oh, that is a good question. (*She smiles at the memory of their favorite activities*) We loved to play a game of hide-and-seek, and we loved to play a game we called "Burglars," where we would hide under the desk in her room and pretend burglars were breaking into the house. My friend Eve would do funny voices and we would run around the house and hide and pretend we were outsmarting the burglars—kind of like *Home Alone*.

Reversing roles, Laurel questioned Mrs. Ramirez about the artifact she had brought. When the interview concluded, Laurel turned to the children.

LAUREL	What did you notice we did to be good listeners for each other?
ERICA	When you were talking to each other you turned your chairs. You did not look to your friends or anything.
LAUREL	Yes, I paid attention to my partner.
RENEE	(*Indicating Mrs. Ramirez*) She was not looking other places, like at the calendar or the books.
LAUREL	Where was Mrs. Ramirez looking?
RENEE	At you.
LAUREL	What did we do to get more information—to learn more about the other person's story?
ALEXIS	You got a lot of ideas because you asked a lot of questions.
LAUREL	Okay! Listen now to directions. To get your partner I am going to give you a card. What is our rule about the cards?
JUAN	That you can't trade because the other person might feel bad.
LAUREL	The other person would feel bad, okay, and we don't want anyone to feel bad. And I have another reason not to switch.
JENNIFER	You want everybody to work with each other in this class!
LAUREL	Right, those are my two reasons.

Laurel's ideas about how children will work with each other were well understood in this class, but it was still early enough in the year to spend a moment to reinforce them. Laurel then distributed cards randomly and set a time limit of about ten minutes for students to interview each other. Children found their match, and the new partners began their interviews at various spots around the room.

JOSÉ   I got a brother and my brother plays with this sometimes. (*He reaches carefully into his bag and pulls out a stuffed rabbit*)

RUDY   Why is it special to you?

JOSÉ   It is special because I got it when I was one year old.

As this interview continued, the video camera visited other partnerships around the room.

PEDRO   I like this because I always play with it and I think because my grandmother gave it to me. She bought it.

GIL   How old were you when your grandmother gave it to you?

PEDRO   Seven.

GIL   Do you have other ones?

PEDRO   No, this is my only one.

GIL   How old was your grandmother when she gave it to you?

PEDRO   Fifty!

As partner interviews concluded, Laurel reminded the class about the second half of their task—drawing a picture of something their partner told them and writing a caption for the picture. Partners shared materials to complete the task, and many discussions continued informally.

AMANDO (*Watching with interest as his partner, Luisa, draws*) My grandfather said that some very nice people used to live in this house. The owner did not want it even though it was very pretty. My grandfather said he would buy it, and the owner sold it to him for three million pesos.

LUISA   (*Looking up in wonder from the picture she is making of Amando's grandfather's house*) Amando! That's a lot!

AMANDO My grandfather said he would pay three million and that was it!

After everyone finished their drawings, each pair of students took a turn sitting in front of the class and explaining what their drawings told about each other. The information they passed along to their classmates showed that they had listened to their partners with genuine interest and respect. Afterwards, Laurel spent a moment helping her students reflect on the activity.

LAUREL   How did you like doing this today? What was it like for you to share something with your partner from home, and did you enjoy learning about what they brought from home?

CYNTHIA   I am glad that we did it.

LAUREL   You are glad? Why?

CYNTHIA   It was fun!

EMILIO   I liked to hear everybody share their picture because it is fun when you see everybody's drawing.

JULIE   I felt a little shy when I was showing my picture about my partner.

SUSANNA   Me, too. I was nervous when I was up there in front of the whole class.

AMANDO   *(With authority)* I liked this activity because people were teaching each other things about what they like at home.

SOME POINTS TO CONSIDER

✔ When children bring something of their lives at home into the classroom, everyone benefits: children see that their experiences outside of school are valued, and they learn new reasons to value each other.

✔ In this particular activity, the objects partners share with each other provide visual help in focusing their conversation—a boon to children who are shy, easily distracted, or, like many of Laurel's students, just learning to speak English.

✔ During class sharing, even the shyer children are willing to show their drawing and tell a little about their partner's artifact—with their partner sitting beside them for support.

✔ And of course, the class sharing provides a way for all children to piece together a little more information about themselves as a community.

Helping Children Get to Know You

THE TEACHERS in this book are active members of their classroom communities, letting students get to know them as learners and people just as they help students get to know each other. Besides participating in structured community-building activities, these teachers also take advantage of the countless informal opportunities that arise in class—to tell a relevant personal story, read a journal entry, offer an opinion in a class discussion, or otherwise share something about themselves.

 **I Hate to Cook**

Becky O'Bryan writes a letter to introduce herself to her grade four-five students. This letter is the first of many ways she signals that she is a fellow member of the classroom community, not just the teacher.

DEAR STUDENTS,

When I was a student, for as long as I can remember, I had trouble sleeping the night before the first day of school. I guess I was wondering what my new teacher would be like, what kind of work I would do, and if I would have friends.

Now that I'm the teacher, I wonder what my new students will be like, what they will think of the activities we do in class, and if they will like me.

So, last night I was very restless—wondering, thinking, and hoping. I know some of you are feeling like me, some worse than me, and some better, but maybe it's reassuring that we are all in the same boat.

I want to tell you about myself. I've been a teacher for 18 years and taught at Auburndale for 15 years. I attended the University of Louisville for my bachelor's and master's degrees. I wanted to be a doctor when I was growing up, and I still might try to do that after I retire from teaching. Lately, I've been thinking about writing a book when I retire, about how teachers can become better teachers. You may have some ideas about that!

I grew up in Louisville very near here. I lived with my mom and two brothers. My older brother was killed in Vietnam in 1967, but my younger brother lives here in Louisville. I attended Jacob Elementary and Iroquois Middle. I went to high school in Simpsonville, Ky. My mother lives in downtown Louisville and I have breakfast with her every Sunday morning.

I've been married 17 years this November and I have a 13-year-old son. He's in the 8th grade and keeps us busy with basketball and baseball, and some tennis. My husband is an insurance representative and he plays tennis. I like sports, especially baseball, but I don't play any. I like to walk and ride my bike. I've wanted to run in the mini-marathon the last couple years, but I didn't get prepared. Even though I'm a U of L graduate, when it comes to U of L vs. U of K rivalry, I don't go for either one.

In my spare time, I enjoy cross-stitching, reading, and hiking. We have been to every state park in Kentucky and many in Indiana. We like to hike the trails. We try to go to Florida every summer. I went to San Francisco this summer and liked the area a lot, although I was worried about earthquakes. There were a few near Los Angeles and Las Vegas the week I was there.

I hate to cook, so don't be surprised to see me out in the many restaurants in our area, especially the pizza places.

I know we'll have a great year, and I'm eager to learn about you in your letters!

Sincerely yours,
Mrs. O'Bryan

A POINT TO CONSIDER

✔ Besides writing this letter on the first day of school, during the next two weeks of school Becky also brought in "a bunch" of pictures of her family and some favorite things to help kids learn more about her. Her students also brought in photos and artifacts, which served as the foundation for a series of partner interviews and writing activities. As the teacher, Becky has the power both to close the distance between herself and her students and to model the value she places on helping everyone get to know each other.

As Laura Havis knows, when children can relate to their teacher as a real person, everyone can relax and a lot more learning can take place.

 ### Dear Mrs. Havis . . . I'm Also Afraid of Thunderstorms

Like Becky and many other teachers, Laura Havis takes time to help her students get to know her. For example, she had all the students in her third-grade class take turns being the "Special Person of the Week." To model the activity for her students and to help them to get to know her, she took the first turn "in the spotlight." She brought photos, objects, and memorabilia that are important to her and displayed them on a bulletin board and a small table; then she talked about her display with children and encouraged their questions.

Like Becky, Laura also incorporates getting-to-know-you activities into her writing program. When she made her "Special Person" presentation, for example, she asked her students to respond by writing letters to her. Their responses indicated not only their interest in getting to know their teacher, but also the powerful ways they found to identify with her as a fellow human being.

Dear Mrs. Havis,

I enjoyed your spotlight. I'm also afraid of thunderstorms
aspcialy at night. I never knew you had children. I also thought
that your spotlight was interesting. I liked your salt and pepper
shakers. Do you have cow and moon salt and pepper shakers?
I think you have a big family.

   It must of been sad for you to know that your dog died.
I know how you feel 2 of my cats got run over by cars. And I'm
still not over that.

          FROM, YOUR STUDENT JESSICA

A POINT TO CONSIDER

✔ When students discover personal connections with their teacher, when they imagine
their teacher as someone with fears or sadnesses or even salt and pepper shakers, it can
increase their desire to please and be like that person. The teachers in this book know
that as they help their students see them as real people working to lead good and productive lives—and dedicated to helping them do the same—they also increase their students' inner drive to be good students and good people.

Getting to Know Your Students

I'T'S OUR JOB to get to know our students. But at the beginning of the year, often all we have to go on are children's official folders of grades, test scores, and previous teachers' evaluations. Beyond the reports of our students' academic past, we have to understand their daily lives, the values and characteristics of their families and neighborhoods, their cultures, their special talents and interests, and perhaps especially, their hopes and dreams.

 **I Don't Have Any Friends**

Laura Ecken makes a conscious effort to understand her individual students, learning much by observing them as they interact with classmates. In an interview with Joan, she described how she gained perspective on one child's behavior.

LAURA   I like to observe the children when they're in partnerships. I'm looking to see how they get along with the other children, what they do when there's a problem, and how they handle it. I'll write little notes about that and then try to structure lessons or activities that take those observations into account.

JOAN   Could you give us an example?

LAURA   For the first few weeks of school I pair students with lots of different random partners, and I have one little girl who couldn't seem to get along with anyone, no matter who she was partnered with. So I set up an activity around "Things I like to do with a friend."

When I checked in with her, she told me she doesn't have any friends. So I asked her, "Can you tell me about that?" What she said was, "My mom and dad don't let me out of the house. I'm not allowed to see anybody or talk to anybody because they'll get me in trouble."

I talked with her parents a little, and I think the child is being perfectly honest. I'll be having a more formal meeting with the parents soon, but I know that I need to do a lot with this child to build friendships in the room, since she's not likely to get opportunities at home.

JOAN   What did you learn when you talked with her parents?

LAURA   Her parents believe that their neighborhood is too dangerous to let her out to play.

SOME POINTS TO CONSIDER

✔ Laura could have made some very wrong assumptions about this child if she hadn't found out more about the girl's home environment. Instead of believing this child to be "difficult," Laura now understands that her student lacks the skills for getting along and being a friend because she has no experience—has not practiced—being a friend.

✔ Laura's culture and background are very different from that of many of her students, which makes it hard for her always to recognize what they bring and anticipate what they may need. She did not, for example, grow up in a neighborhood where it was dangerous for children to play outside. But Laura understands her responsibility, given these differences, to make an extra effort to find out what she doesn't know and try to understand what she might otherwise misunderstand.

✔ Because Laura made it a point to find out more about this child, she now has a connection with the girl's parents and can express to them her concerns about their child's limited social opportunities.

✔ And because of what she knows about this student's home situation, Laura can consciously shape the girl's classroom experience to help her develop the ability to be a friend—an ability that will be as important to her in becoming a productive member of society as anything else she may ever learn in school.

 I Feel a Chart Coming On!

A powerful aspect of getting to know students involves building connections to their lives at home. As teacher Dawn Biscardi observes, "Children sometimes separate the idea of family and school, so I think it's a good idea to create a caring family *between* home and school."

Dawn has a reputation in her class for listing and charting everything. Her third-graders have even taken to trilling "I feel a chart coming on!" When Joan visited Dawn's classroom, she found that the charts posted everywhere were actually one of the ways Dawn communicates with parents about the tenor and specifics of life in their children's classroom.

JOAN   You must have a special reason for all these charts I see around the room. Could you explain?

DAWN   We make charts of what we value and what we're learning, and we post them around the room. But we also frequently type them up and send them home. I say to parents, "You might want to make these into charts and stick them around the house. These charts help remind children of what we value and that what's going on in school is a process that doesn't stop here."

Some of my children have told me that they have these charts at home all over their room, and I think, "Good! Good! Good!" I believe that the more concrete examples we can give them of what they learn, the more they'll hang on to that learning and own it.

JOAN   So when the charts go home, you really have two audiences in mind, the children and their parents?

DAWN   My goal is to build a team between school and home. I want to pull in every aspect of what happens in the classroom for the parents—for their knowledge and for their involvement. Children are far more invested, I believe, in becoming serious learners when they know their parents are supportive and behind them.

I want the parents as well as the children to understand that "We are in this thing together." So we share the experiences and the learning and the good things— together!

A POINT TO CONSIDER

✔ The notion that "we are in this together" permeates Dawn's classroom, and she helps everyone understand that "we" all do better when information is shared and when relationships—in class and with children's homes—are nurtured.

■

In this chapter we have visited teachers who understand the crucial role of fostering caring relationships in order to build a classroom learning community. They have shown us the importance of planning carefully to invite all students into the community—even sitting in the chairs of individual children to help imagine their perspective, as Louise does. We have been urged to make time for students to learn about each other and how to work together, and we have been assured that the time invested is worth it—that students' increased comfort and confidence in the classroom results in powerful long-term learning gains. And finally, we have seen teachers who understand the role of adults in a caring learning community—both their own role as a model and participant, and the role of the children's parents as informed and involved supporters.

In the next chapter, we will learn about some of the ways teachers help their students understand and practice the bedrock values that lead to harmonious classrooms and humane societies.

Teaching Humane Values

"SOME RED FLAGS WENT UP FOR ME RIGHT AWAY— teaching values? Values are taught in homes and churches." Like teacher Marcia Davis, many of us have worried about what it means to "teach values." But as Marcia observed on reflection, children experience values in school every day in many, many ways, beginning with the behaviors and activities we emphasize in the classroom, the ways we respond to even the most challenging students, and the ways we treat other adults in the school. Because values are communicated all the time in schools, why not be explicit about what those values are and deliberate in letting the kids in on it?

Helping Children Establish Class Norms

THE IMPORTANCE of the social and ethical values that children experience in the classroom—the values that are modeled and lived there—cannot be overemphasized: children need to experience fairness, respect, helpfulness, responsibility, kindness, and consideration in order to reciprocate such behavior. But in addition, children need our guidance in talking about *why* these values are important, understanding *how* these values relate to specific behaviors, and recognizing how to *apply* these values broadly—within and beyond the classroom walls.

An effective first step in teaching values is to have students recognize what values are important to them and why. "How do you want others to treat you?" is a question that implies—even to elementary students—reciprocity. To expect to be treated in ways that are respectful, kind, courteous, helpful, considerate, fair, and responsible means being someone who treats others in these ways. In a classroom setting, we might ask, "What are the ways we want our class to be?"

If we want to establish a caring learning environment that fosters and depends on children's intrinsic motivation rather than our external coercion, what strategies help?

 In My Perfect School People Aren't Calling You Names All the Time

Bringing children's conscious attention to the values they hold for themselves and others begins in the first weeks of the school year. In Carole Lewis's grade five-six class, we can see how she worked over the course of three class meetings to co-create class norms with her students so that they can organize their behavior around principles, not just rules.*

Session One

> From her place on the floor, Carole looked around the circle of children, acknowledged the heat of the September afternoon, and introduced the topic of the class meeting.
>
> CAROLE   I'd like to talk about how we want it to go for the rest of the year, because it's us in a room, for six hours a day.

---

* Excerpted from DSC Video Library, "September."

Carole then invited the children to close their eyes and visualize themselves coming to school. In a measured voice she asked a series of questions to focus the children's attention on how people in their "perfect" school would be treated.

CAROLE   Imagine yourself as you open the classroom door . . . and maybe you're a little late . . . How do you see the teacher receiving you? . . . How do you see your classmates receiving you? . . . When it's time to go out to recess, do you have a place to go? . . . Are there people to play with? To talk to? . . . What about lunch time, do you have people to eat with? . . . What happens when you come up to a table . . . and maybe it's a little crowded? . . . This is your perfect school . . . how do you want it to be?

Okay, slowly open your eyes . . . Did you make a good world . . . a good place for yourself?

Carole went on to explain that students would now talk with a partner about how they wanted their perfect school to look and feel. Each partnership would then agree on one, two, or three ideas to record on sentence strips and to post for later class discussion. Ideas from three partnerships are captured below.

DANIEL   It looks like not calling you names all the time, and if they don't like you, just keep it to themselves.

B. K.   Yeah, keep it to yourself. So, let's see, how could we phrase that? Caring about other people's feelings?

——

TERESA   What if we write "rude" and we put a circle and a cross through it, like they have in the "no smoking" signs?

TIFFANY   Yeah. I was embarrassed today when I was eating lunch with my friends and then I bent down to get something and when I got up I flipped somebody's Coke can over and all the kids sort of laughed.

——

JAMES   What you're trying to say is you would like people not to say that you're showing off and stuff?

STEVEN   Yeah, and not pick on me.

The sentence strips from these and other partnerships came to fill a double expanse of blackboard with students' heartfelt ideas about ways they wanted their class to be. Carole asked students to be thinking for their class meeting the next day about what their ideas had in common and what categories they might fall into.

Session Two

Children were seated on the floor reading and pointing to the sentence strips they had previously posted on the board.

CAROLE Take a minute and look over what we put up yesterday. Do you see any similarities or any groupings?

DANIEL Things like "respect" and "helping."

CAROLE Okay, could you put some of the "respect" things all together?

Carole wrote the headings "Respect" and "Helping" on the board, and Daniel and a few other students moved several of the sentence strips under "Respect."

CAROLE What other categories do you see?

CELESTE People shouldn't be mean.

CAROLE Okay, what would that go under? What would we call it?

TWO VOICES "Caring."

CAROLE Do you agree?

SEVERAL VOICES Yeah, "caring."

MEREDITH I think there should be a category for "friends."

CAROLE What could we call that?

SEVERAL VOICES "Friendship."

When children seemed satisfied with the categories of "Respect," "Helping," "Caring," and "Friendship," Carole invited them to position the rest of sentence strips under an appropriate heading.

CAROLE If you think of something that isn't up here, there's still paper. We could still put it up. But these look like our basic goals, and tomorrow we're going to talk about what the heck we're going to do about it.

Session Three

Pairs of students have prepared for the meeting by talking with each other about how the class norms can be put to use. Carole and the children have seated themselves in a circle on the floor.

CAROLE   What if there's a problem—what do you want to have happen? How can our norms help us?

MEREDITH   We thought if you put all the ideas down on one piece of paper that we would put a little row for checking names off if you didn't do it.

CAROLE   Like for yourself? When you are not doing the idea, you check it? And what would the check do for you?

MEREDITH   Well, it will remind you. Like, the teacher will give the reminder, and if you did it again, then the teacher will come and check it off.

CAROLE   I would do that? Do you think the teacher should be the one to be in charge of this?

MEREDITH   No. Like, maybe your partner could, if she thought you were fooling around or something.

CAROLE   How would you feel if your sheet was there and somebody was checking it?

MEREDITH   Well, they would give a reminder . . .

CAROLE   How? Pretend it's me. I'm goofing off.

MEREDITH   Carole, would you please stop goofing off, I'm trying to learn.

CAROLE   I'm not goofing off!

MEREDITH   Well, it seems to me like you are.

CAROLE   *(Coming out of role)* Okay, then what would you do at that point with this sheet?

MEREDITH   Well, I would just give you a gentle reminder, and then if you kept on doing it, I would tell the teacher.

CAROLE   So the reminder was verbal?

MEREDITH   Yeah. And then if you kept on doing it after a gentle reminder, I would tell the teacher and they would come and put a check on the paper.

CAROLE   Thank you. *(Turning to the whole group)* When you're in trouble—if you're bugging somebody, because we all bug somebody sometime—do you want my role to be to get you in trouble or to come and help solve?

STEVEN   I would want you to help solve, because it would be better on the kids, because if you tell them, that person's going to hold it against you.

JOHN   I want personally ideas to help us settle it.

CAROLE   So, what would you do if that was your situation and you had asked the person and reminded them, and you wanted some help?

JOHN   I would probably come to you and say, "Can we have some ideas on how to settle this problem?"

CAROLE   So you would ask the teacher? Let's go back to Meredith and let's make it "Jesse's bugging you."

MEREDITH   Oh, no. *(Jesse, who was sitting next to Meredith, grinned in anticipation)*

CAROLE   So, Jesse's bugging you and you've reminded him. Now you're going to come to the teacher.

MEREDITH   Mrs. Lewis, Jesse's bugging me. Could you please give me some ideas to tell Jesse to please stop, because he's not letting me listen.

CAROLE   So you're asking for help? Am I the only one in this room?

ELISE   If a person is bothering you and your friend is closer than you are, maybe they could help. Like if I'm in a fight with someone and I get Celeste because she's closer?

CAROLE   What would you say to Celeste?

ELISE   Celeste, can you help me because she's bothering me and I would like you to help me.

By role-playing ways to solve problems, the students in Carole Lewis's class "try on" ways to take more responsibility and honor their class norms.

CAROLE Okay. Who's involved in the problem?

ELISE Us.

CAROLE Who does Celeste need to help?

ELISE Both of us.

CAROLE Can you phrase it that way?

ELISE Can you help both of us because we're both having a problem.

CAROLE How does that sound? If you're the one that people are angry with?

SAMI I would want people to understand my position, 'cause if I was being mean to them there would have to be a reason.

CAROLE Okay . . . pretend you and Jerome are having a problem. What would be the first thing you would do?

SAMI I would go up to him and ask him, like, to stop doing whatever he's doing that's annoying. It's like, "Don't push me, ask me." Like, if I tell him meanly, "Stop," and he won't stop because I was being mean to him. But if I said it nicely and respected him he would stop.

CAROLE Is that true, Jerome?

JEROME Probably.

CAROLE And then you're not in trouble.

JEROME Yeah.

CAROLE "In trouble" is such a bad word, isn't it?

SOME POINTS TO CONSIDER

✔ Carole's intention in these meetings was not for children to arrive at a particular set of class agreements or norms, but for them to see that values such as respect and fairness are not the arbitrary inventions of adults. Children nominated their own authentic values—the ways *they* want their class to be, the principles that would help them, for example, avoid picking on each other or calling each other names.

✔ The commitment that children have to uphold those class norms which they develop themselves is very different from any commitment to a set of class rules Carole might simply announce. Instead, children had extended opportunities for reflection and input, including their first imaginings of a "perfect" school, partner discussions about what such a school would look and feel like, and class meetings to arrive at widespread understandings and agreements.

✔ Carole's role in helping children arrive at those understandings was significant. She asked questions that helped children see the ramifications of some of their ideas, she role-played with them to further clarify their thinking, and she helped them rehearse ways they could act on their own behalf.

✔ In addition to helping children see that they *could* act on their own behalf, Carole helped them understand why they *should*—why being able to solve their own problems rather than depending on "the teacher" would help them feel more mature and responsible.

 ## I Used to Be Heavy-handed

The children in Carole Lewis's class are ten and eleven years old, old enough to think about behavior in abstract terms such as respect and responsibility. What about younger children, who think more concretely and who have less experience negotiating social behavior? Can young children also be helped to co-create class norms that are personally meaningful? In the interview below, Marcia Davis described the considerations that went into the co-creation of class norms with her grade two-three students.

JOAN Would you explain how you came to use "friendship" to help children develop class norms?

MARCIA In past years I talked with children about how we wanted our class to be—with some heavy-handed guidance of the discussion by me—and I used to sum up the discussion by composing three rules. Children accepted these, but didn't feel the ownership they do when they're allowed to have more input.

This year I delayed norm-setting with my children until three weeks into the school year. Instead, we began with a whole lot of different activities with a friendship theme, because friendship is something my children could connect to. Delaying the norm-setting gave us time to have shared experiences and establish that we're all friends in our classroom.

When we got around to setting norms, we did lots of talking about how friends work together and treat each other. As we talked, strong feelings were generated about how we wanted to be treated and how we wanted our class to be. I built on this by connecting the children's past experiences to these feelings and discussing how we feel when something bad happens and how we can handle it if it happens in our class.

After lots of partner sharing and class discussion, we posted three charts, with the headings "Ways We Are Kind," "Our Responsibilities," and "Fairness." Then children wrote on them the specific things that tell us that we are acting in those ways in our classroom. The chart-making allowed everyone to have input as we built a knowledge base together. We talked about why behaving in those ways was important.

JOAN   After children listed specific actions that illustrate values, how did you use those charts?

MARCIA   We left the charts displayed around the room to keep the ideas in front of us and to be able to refer to or review them. We also made a chart showing our "Successes and Rough Spots." As we were able to move things from the "Rough Spots" column to the "Successes" column, we had visible proof of our growth as a class, and it reinforced the concept that we're always in the process of moving and changing as a group.

When we created our class norms this year, I was surprised yet again at how much wisdom, insight, and sensitivity children possess—and how earnest they are in wanting to be part of a fair and responsible class. When we studied the Pilgrims' signing of the Mayflower Compact, we tied it into the signing of our class norms. Each of us signed our name at the bottom of the chart—the children took it very seriously.

SOME POINTS TO CONSIDER

✔ Marcia gave her young students lots of experiences working together and thinking about friendship before she asked them to apply those experiences to the job of co-creating class norms. In this way children's concrete experiences and sharply remembered feelings helped them understand and take the job to heart.

✔ By acknowledging the inevitability of "rough spots" and the attainability of "successes," Marcia helped children see behavior as something they would be getting better at—making mistakes along the way, perhaps, but learning.

✔ Children's class norms didn't just get created and then set aside. They remained posted and easy to refer to, and the two-column "Successes and Rough Spots" chart changed as the children did.

✔ Marcia and the other teachers who have helped to create this book know that teaching about values doesn't stop with a list of class norms. Because children need time to build and deepen their understandings of any significant concepts, these teachers take time throughout the year to help children reflect on their class norms and evaluate how well they are living by them.

Collaborative Learning — A Laboratory for Applying Values

SINCE PRACTICE IS a basic strategy for getting better at anything, it makes sense to give children lots of direct practice applying values. Structured group activities can be an important way to help children practice values such as fairness, helping, respect, and responsibility. The deliberate introduction of social as well as academic goals for an activity, the availability of adult guidance should a situation become too difficult for children to handle on their own, and the deliberate reflection by students on how well they met the activity's social and academic goals—these characteristics distinguish structured activities from the informal opportunities children also have to practice applying values.

 Nobody Took Over Other People

In Terry Rice's sixth grade, children encountered their first structured collaborative activity four days into the school year. As Terry introduced the concept of alliteration and how students could use it in writing a group poem using all of their names, he also spent time having students anticipate how "respect for others" and "responsibility," which he had written on the board as broad social goals, might be important during their group work.

TERRY   Respect for others—what do we mean by that if a group is working on a poem together?

SHARON   Don't make fun of people.

MONIQUE When you make up an alliteration name for a person make it not a mean one.

TERRY   Yes—it needs to be positive. What about responsibility? What do we mean by responsibility?

SHARON Get your work done.

SANDEEP Do not fool around.

JOHN   Be responsible with the materials.

TERRY   What are you going to need in your group to write your poem? How are you going to do this?

JOHN   Will we have a big piece of paper or a small one?

TERRY   You need to decide that in your group. You also might want to think about things like is somebody going to have to write this down and is somebody going to have to report to the class. You will need to figure out ways to share responsibility.

Groups moved off to their tables, but two groups in particular took quite a while to work out how they would tackle the task and who would do what. Terry moved about the room, observing and acting as a resource by asking questions or simply listening.

Eventually all groups became productively engaged, and as poems neared completion, Terry gave an index card to each group and asked them to write about *how* they met the social goals of showing respect for everyone in the group and acting responsibly.

Jeanne, Maria, Sandeep, and Sharon completed their reflection card and showed it to Terry, satisfied that they had achieved their social goals. But since they had simply restated the broad goals to treat each other with respect and to be responsible, Terry asked them to consider *how* they achieved their goals. Their completed card was quite specific!

WE SHOWED RESPECT TO EACH OTHER
    excepting each others ideas
    nobody took over other people

WE SHARED WORK EVENLY
    we all thought of words
    we took turns
    shared ideas

WE WERE RESPONSIBLE
    by helping each other
    we did not fight
    no screaming

BY JEANNE, MARIA, SANDEEP, AND SHARON

After the poems and cards were completed, a representative from each group read the group's alliterative poem to the class. When both Monique and Russell got up to share from one group, Russell explained how their group solved a potential problem.

RUSSELL   We were fighting over who was going to do it, and our group said, "Why don't you both do it? Two people can read for the group." So we are.

After Russell and Monique read, Terry moved students into a discussion of the activity's social goals.

TERRY   Monique and Russell, I want to ask you guys about your group's social goals—what you have on your index card.

MONIQUE   We wrote: "We were cooperative and we worked together as a team. We did have problems on spelling."

TERRY   What did you do to resolve that?

MONIQUE   We used a dictionary.

TERRY   How did you share responsibility?

MONIQUE   We all did something and we all thought about other people's names.

TERRY   I also heard when I was at your table the idea that if you two reported for your group this time, then someone else could have a turn next time.

LORRAINE   In our group we got along really good and we argued politely. There were no put-downs.

TERRY   So you disagreed in a nice way. That is important. If you do not feel something is right you should say so, but you say it in a nice way.

GERALDO   In our group we wrote: "We were responsible by helping out each other and being kind, generous, and thoughtful. We had no put-downs. We worked at including everybody." *(Parenthetically)* We had a problem with that at the start.

TERRY   Why do you think it's important to work in ways that are respectful and responsible?

TIFFANY   We do not want people to hurt each other.

AMANDA   And we should have a good reputation.

JOHN   It helps you find out about each other.

ALANA   Being responsible and doing your share of the work helps you get a good education for when you leave school and get a job.

RUSSELL   If you do not want to be treated bad, you do not treat somebody else bad. What goes around comes around.

SOME POINTS TO CONSIDER

✔ Terry did a number of things to assist children's prosocial development. He introduced clear social goals before children actually worked in their small groups, and he asked them to think about what respect and responsibility might mean in the context of their upcoming work together.

✔ He monitored groups carefully, but rather than intervene to tell them how to proceed, he acted as a resource to help children work things out for themselves.

✔ In preparation for reflection time, Terry gave students a few minutes to write specific ideas on index cards about how their group worked together toward their social goals. During the reflection discussion, Terry helped children articulate *why* it is important to work in ways that are responsible and respectful, knowing that children are more likely to build commitment to ideas whose purpose they understand.

✔ The social goals and related skills that students discussed in Terry's class are only two among many particular behaviors that teachers or students might identify to work on (see the chart, "Examples of Collaborative Skills Related to Values," on the following page). Throughout the year, with a variety of activities, Terry will help children focus on many of these behaviors, depending on which ones are most relevant to their particular needs.

Examples of Collaborative Skills
Related to Values

FAIRNESS	RESPONSIBILITY	CONCERN AND RESPECT FOR OTHERS	HELPFULNESS
Equal Participation • asking questions to get everyone's ideas, opinions, and feelings • taking turns • letting everyone have a chance to talk • making sure everyone has a job or part of the task • sharing materials **Fair Decision Making** • getting all opinions before making a decision • choosing a fair way to decide • supporting the group's agreement or decision	• stating your ideas, opinions, and feelings • asking questions to get a clear understanding • asking others in your group for help when you need it • putting forth extra effort when necessary • letting others know when you disagree and why • making sure you do your part of the work • doing your best • helping the group stay focused on the work • following the ground rules for cooperative group work	• making suggestions without being bossy • listening to the person who is talking • encouraging differing opinions • being sensitive to different abilities and needs • disagreeing in a respectful way • expressing appreciation and support for others' ideas and work	• checking to make sure others understand (the task, question, or answer) • showing or explaining without doing the other person's work • taking a part when someone has a job that is too big or too hard

If They Are Locked in the Bathroom You Can Help Them Get Out

In collaborative classrooms, helping is a value everyone gets to practice—a lot. In the scene below, Louise Lotz's first-graders spent some time with their second-grade buddies from Mrs. Fererra's class talking about helping and then practicing a bit of it.

After welcoming the second-graders, Louise asked them to take the hand of their first-grade buddy and come sit on the carpet.

LOUISE   We are going to be talking together in partnerships about ways that you can help each other. That can be in the yard, in the lunchroom, or in the classroom. We have been talking about this today in first grade, and we have been talking about what it means to be friends together. This morning, in the yard, I saw some second-graders helping first-graders, and I did not even have to ask them.

Ben, what is one way you can help?

BEN   If someone is sick you can take them into the office.

GAYLE   If they get something in their throat, you can push their stomach up so they can breathe.

LOUISE   Okay, that might be something you want to get the yard duty teacher for.

BRODY   If they are locked in the bathroom you can help them get out. ·

CLARISSA   You can help them by flushing the toilet.

MRS.
FERRERA   Somebody made me feel good when I was looking sad because they came up and gave me a smile.

Modeling with Mrs. Ferrera as her buddy, Louise demonstrated the "helping hands" interview partners would do together, the tracing each child would make of his or her partner's hand, and the drawing each child would then make inside the tracing about a way his or her partner did something helpful.

LOUISE   When everyone is finished we are going to go out in the hallway and put the pictures along the walls so we can remember how we are going to help. How many second-graders remember doing this last year? (*Many hands go up*) So, there are lots of second-graders who can help if you are not sure what to do. There are a lot of people in here, so half of the people are going with Mrs. Ferrera and half will stay here. Mrs. Fererra's classroom is right behind this wall. If we knock, she can hear us. She is real close.

Half of the children went off with Mrs. Fererra, and Louise moved among the remaining partnerships, reminding children (as needed) to put the crayons away and do their talking first. Kyle and Matt had not begun the task and were playing with Matt's small plastic toys instead. Louise knelt by the pair.

KYLE   We're having trouble thinking.

LOUISE   Remember when we sat in a circle this morning? What were some of the ways we said we help each other?

MATT   *(Shrugs)*

LOUISE   What do you do to help at home?

MATT   Well, I clean my room.

LOUISE   And that's a way you can help in this class, too, when it's time to clean up. Kyle, how do you think you might help someone on the playground?

KYLE   *(Shrugs)*

LOUISE   What if someone is walking along and looks sad, all by themselves?

KYLE   Give them a hug?

MATT   Ask them to play with us.

LOUISE   You have given me some ideas and I have given you some ideas. Do you think you can decide now what you are going to draw?

BOYS   *(Both nod)*

LOUISE   *(Gathering up the small plastic toys)* Do you mind if I hang on to these till we finish?

MATT   Okay.

Louise moved on, stopping to talk with Tanya and Lauren.

LOUISE   What did you decide to draw?

TANYA   We can help each other read. We are pretending we are twins and so we are going to do the same picture.

Across the room, a group of three was having trouble. Mitchell was sitting apart from Lauren and Cooper, who were busy working on their drawings. Mitchell had an empty tracing of Cooper's hand in front of him.

COOPER   What's the matter, Mitchell?

MITCHELL I want to draw what you told me, but I don't know how.

Cooper went across the room and asked Louise what he should do.

LOUISE   Can you think of a way of helping Mitchell draw without doing it all for
          him?

When Louise checked later with the trio, she found that Cooper had drawn part of the picture for Mitchell, and Mitchell was pasting a small self-portrait onto the picture to complete it. Mitchell looked much happier, as Cooper sat nearby reading and watching him finish up.

COOPER   Good job!

SOME POINTS TO CONSIDER

✔ In this activity, the focus on helping is quite explicit. Louise gets children thinking about ways they help in school and at home, and then she structures a collaborative activity in which the practice of helping is unavoidable: partners must tell each other about a helping experience, cooperate in the tracing of each other's hand, and help to see that each drawing is completed.

✔ When all the pictures are mounted on the wall outside the two classrooms, the completed mural of "Ways We Help" provides visual evidence for the children that they are people who want to be helpful and know how to do it!

Spontaneous Learning and Teaching about Values

IN ADDITION TO structured activities that focus children on specific values, each day in the classroom offers hundreds of informal opportunities to teach children about values. All of the many ways we interact with our students as we work to keep our classrooms peaceful and productive are powerful teaching opportunities.

When our focus shifts from simply controlling the classroom to helping children take responsibility for their own behavior, our entire classroom management system is, in fact, about teaching values.

Who Can Tell Me What Your Responsibilities Are in This Group?

In a partner activity about kindness, third-grade teacher Dawn Biscardi seized on a spontaneous opportunity to help one group focus first on responsibility.

> On the previous day partners had interviewed each other about ways they are kind at home. Now Dawn has asked pairs to interview each other about ways they could be kind at school. Chonte, Maria, and Itzel formed a threesome since Itzel's partner was absent.

CHONTE   You gotta ask me a question!

MARIA   I did!

CHONTE   Well, I did not give the answer!

ITZEL   What would you say when somebody was beating up someone?

MARIA   What would you do when somebody is sick?

ITZEL   *(Answering her own question)* You would say, "Sorry, I did not mean it."

Having observing quietly from a distance, Dawn moved over to ask a question.

DAWN   Who can tell me what your responsibilities are in this group? What should you be doing at this point?

ITZEL   We should be talking to our partners about how they are nice, but it is hard because there are three of us and I was going to do *her* next.

MARIA   I was doing Chonte first and then I was going to do Itzel.

DAWN   What do we need to think about when we have a group of three people?

CHONTE   How we can all get to ask questions and give answers.

MARIA   Taking turns.

ITZEL   Waiting.

DAWN   I'll tell you what I'm going to do. I am going to step back and listen to see how you three children figure out how you can all get to say something in the next few minutes. See what you can do about fixing it so that everybody feels they have had a turn.

MARIA   Itzel, what do you do if your friend does not have a boyfriend?

ITZEL   I do not know.

MARIA   Well, I will tell you. I would share with them. Now it's your turn.

ITZEL   Chonte, what would you do if someone was fighting with your best friend?

CHONTE   I would stop them from fighting.

A few questions later, Dawn checked in with the group.

DAWN   How are you doing?

MARIA   Great!

DAWN   One thing I noticed—when you think of a question for your partner, should you also give them the answer?

MARIA   *(Abashedly)* Not really.

DAWN   What could you do so that your partner thinks of an answer?

SOME POINTS TO CONSIDER

✔ Dawn felt that Maria, Chonte, and Itzel were stuck in an unproductive muddle, so she intervened. She asked a question that kept the students thinking about their role— "Who can tell me what your responsibilities are in this group?"—rather than a question about the teacher's role—such as, "What did I ask you to do?" She helped students reclaim responsibility for their own learning.

✔ Even after she left the group, Dawn stayed aware of their progress and checked back in with them. Her final two questions to this group—"When you think of a question for your partner, should you give them the answer?" and "What can you do so that your partner thinks of an answer?"—helped the girls reflect both on their responsibilities in a collaborative learning context and on how to struggle with and practice *being* responsible.

Kindergarten *Is* Cooperation

We have visited classrooms where sixth-graders, third-graders, and even second- and first-graders were practicing the values embedded in collaborative activities. But what about kindergartners? It is not unusual to hear kindergarten teachers say, as Maria Vallejo once did, "Oh, we can't do collaborative learning. My children are just too egocentric."

In the following visit to Maria's classroom, now that she is in the middle of her second year of pairing kindergartners for collaborative learning, we can see not only that she has structured many ways for children to practice values as they collaborate formally and informally, but that her kindergarten embodies cooperation.

Children were engaged in a variety of activities, both in the classroom and out in the courtyard. Maria sat at the writing table with Rafael, who had just "written" in his journal about his drawing of E.T. "Does E.T. miss home?" Maria wrote back. Brittany put a box of pencils down on the table beside Rafael.

BRITTANY You gotta share these, okay?

In the book corner, Deveau and Aaron were sharing a book about motorcycles.

AARON I got a real motorcycle.

DEVEAU At your home?

AARON Yep, in my garage.

DEVEAU Do you ride it?

AARON Yep, in the daytime and in the nighttime.

At the easel, Kyle added a chimney to his artwork. Brittany stopped by to look, pointing at a boy in a car.

BRITTANY Good boy. But there's no wheels.

Brittany took up a crayon and added the wheels; Kyle colored them in. Then Brittany began to add another face in the car.

KYLE No, I don't want it.

Brittany ignored him.

KYLE *(Emphatically)* No, I don't want it!

Brittany still ignored Kyle, who then left the easel and went to join Mrs. Baker, the aide, and two children who were about to read a book.

MARIA *(Singing to signal time to come together on the mat)* The more we get together, together, together . . .

When everyone had gathered, Tawnee began with a question to Maria. Brittany raised her hand insistently. When Maria finished answering Tawnee, she turned to the class.

MARIA If you have your hand up while someone is talking, that is saying to them, "Please hurry up, I have something to say." How does that make them feel?

Maria Vallejo's kindergarten students represent a range of developmental levels, but each child is capable of contributing to a collaborative classroom.

JAIME   Sad.

CARL   Not good.

MARIA   I think so too. We are not showing respect that way.

Maria reached over to turn on a tape. The children wriggled with pleasure as they sang along and read the Spanish-language big book *De Colores*. At the conclusion of the tape, Deveau spoke for many of his classmates.

DEVEAU   We want to dance together!

After a few minutes of joyful dancing, Maria settled the children down and explained that half of the learning partners would now go with Mrs. Baker, to do an activity connected to the work the class had been doing on "feelings." Maria explained that each child would be listening to his or her partner and drawing what the partner was afraid of.

MARIA   If Grinda is my partner, will I draw what I am afraid of, or what Grinda is afraid of?

CHORUS   Grinda!

When half the learning partnerships had left to join Mrs. Baker, Maria introduced a cooperative sorting activity to the remaining partnerships.

MARIA   The other day when we were sorting, we used buttons. Today, we have boxes with different things in them. I am going to put one of these out, and I am going to pretend that Eric is my learning partner. When I pick, I am going to find two things that are the same, and then Eric is going to find two for himself that are the same.

Eric watched Maria place two objects from the box on the mat, and then he chose his two.

MARIA   Is he going to do them all, or am I going to do some?

BILLY   You take turns.

MARIA   Why?

BILLY   Because we are learning partners and we have to help each other out.

MARIA   Whose turn is it to pick now?

SEVERAL
VOICES   Eric's.

Eric and Maria continued their sorting, modeling how to take turns very clearly. Then learning partnerships spread out to investigate the contents of their boxes.

DEVEAU   We got beads! Okay, you pick first.

AARON   No, you pick first.

—

TAWNEE   We got keys! This is my side and that is your side.

CHERYL   Okay. I will sort the silver ones and you sort the gold.

—

COREY   Don't dump them, Eric! Put them carefully.

ERIC   It is my turn to pick . . . What ones do you want?

Maria moved among the partnerships, observing, questioning, giving feedback, and encouraging children to reflect.

MARIA   I noticed the way Rosa was handing the keys to you, Marla. That was help-ful to your partnership . . . What is another way we could sort them? What if I put these together?

ROSA   Oh, that's a good idea!

Eric and Corey remained engaged in sorting their tiny teddy bears long after other part-nerships had cleaned up and moved on to other activities. Yvette interrupted the pair.

YVETTE   It's restaurant time. You have to come.

COREY   We have to clean up first.

YVETTE   Want me to help you?

COREY   No, we can do it.

Quickly cleaning up, the two boys went off to the restaurant, where Yvette and Miguel served them grape juice and crackers. As Eric and Corey enjoyed their snack, Yvette crossed their names off the restaurant list and Miguel organized more snacks for the next learning partnership on the list.

Outside, Kristy and Juan shoveled and dug in the sand tray. Cesar watched enviously.

CESAR   You don't like girls.

JUAN   Yep, I like girls now.

CESAR   You like her?

JUAN   Yep.

Seeing that Kristy could not be dislodged, Cesar took up a shovel and joined in the creation of a "hill" in the middle of the tray. Quite a lot of sand disappeared over the side as the pile grew.

MARIA   Can you move back and look? What can you see?

JUAN   Yikes!

Wordlessly, each child worked to shovel the sand back into the tray.

SOME POINTS TO CONSIDER

✔ There is a quality of self-regulation among the children in Maria's kindergarten. They not only know the routines of the classroom, they also know there is leeway for them to suggest an impromptu dance or to stay a little longer with an activity they find particularly engaging or challenging.

✔ Whether demonstrating how to take turns sorting, or commenting on a helpful interaction between partners, or asking children to reflect on how it feels to be interrupted by a waving hand, or assuming that spilled sand will mean the same thing to the children at the sand tray as it does to her, Maria works consistently to point out ways children are and can be fair, kind, helpful, and responsible.

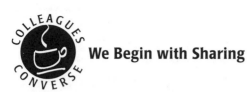 **We Begin with Sharing**

The scene described above is one that Maria worked hard to achieve. There are still occasional problems and children whose development is less advanced than others, but that's just normal. The question is, how did Maria work with her students over the course of the year to put values at the center of all their interactions?

JOAN   It's evident to me that your children have had a great deal of practice and some very skillful guidance in order to get to this point. I know it didn't just happen. What are some of the informal things you do with your kindergartners to introduce them to the idea of a collaborative classroom?

MARIA   We begin with sharing informally. For example, by having a tub of crayons on a table where four children sit, they learn to share, and we talk about how we share. Later, you see they are doing little things like taking a basket of materials and putting it between two children rather than keeping it to themselves. You see children bringing in a little bag of Cheerios to share . . . and children who recognize what isn't fair . . . and children who are learning to negotiate.

Sharing food is a way to help children learn many things. Over food, people bond! Our restaurant operates every day, and each partnership gets a turn to prepare snacks for the other children. Every Friday we cook, and we always have a tablecloth with flowers and napkins. The children serve each other and then sit next to each other. This gives us opportunities to talk about courtesy—for example, waiting for your partner to finish—or responsibility—like cleaning up after yourself.

Every time we clean up, it's an opportunity to model and talk about helping. A classroom where children are helping each other is so peaceful!

They are also learning how to take turns and solve problems. I try to help children learn responsibility. If there is a problem I ask, "What is the problem? How can you solve it?" I model that a lot, and I sometimes have to help children with the language of what to say to each other, suggesting a question they could ask or a statement they could make. They don't always have the language to know what to say.

JOAN   When did you start putting children together in partnerships? How did that work?

MARIA First we started with informal partnerships, lots of random grouping for simple rhymes and singing and chanting games where they needed a partner—and even for walking in line outside with a partner. That was the beginning of learning to be with one other person. Then about four months into the year we began our formal learning partnerships. Children also had been cooperating with their third-grade buddies, which gave them a positive picture of what partnerships looked like.

Another thing I'm doing this year for formal partner learning is to send half of the group off with Mrs. Baker and keep the other half with me. I also keep partners together for a long time once we get past the early random pairings. Children have had the same learning partner for two months now and I am just about ready to change them.

Next year I will start everything a lot earlier now that I have worked out ways to gradually build these partnerships. I believe in them—I have seen them be quite successful. One little girl said to me the other day, "You help us learn." And I said back, "You help each other learn." Another child piped up, "Like our learning partners—they help us learn—that's why we have them!"

A POINT TO CONSIDER

✔ As Maria's five-year-olds demonstrate, practicing and learning about values does not have to come at the expense of academic learning. With conscious attention, we can integrate children's social, ethical, and academic learning—and achieve more, not less, overall learning.

Using Literature to Highlight Values

IN ADDITION TO understanding how values apply in their classrooms, children need opportunities to see the relationship between what they are learning in class and how it plays out in the broader world. Children's literature is a powerful way to help them see this.

Through literature children see values applied in a multitude of contexts—both familiar and unfamiliar. They see that human values, needs, and motivations are universal. And by examining the choices made by characters in literature, children can rehearse some of the choices they may have to make in their own lives—choices about how to behave with principle and with consideration for others.

How Do You Think Abbie Felt When Her Father Left?

In the scene described below, first-grade partners in Nancy Day Chapel's classroom consider "responsibility" from the perspective of a nineteenth-century girl their age as well as from their own twentieth-century perspective.

> The children sat quietly as Nancy finished reading the true story of Abbie, a girl whose father depended on her to keep the lighthouse lights burning in a frightening emergency. As the children's spontaneous comments about the story trailed off, Nancy asked the children to make a connection between Abbie's responsibilities and the work each of them would be doing next with their reading partners.

NANCY   What responsibilities do you have to each other when we do a "partner read"? How will your partner be depending on you?

BETH   We read the story.

DANIEL   And we ask questions

NANCY   How do you decide who reads?

CODY   Well, we take turns. We can read a paragraph each.

JESSICA   Or a page each.

NANCY   When one person is reading, what is the responsibility of the other person?

SEVERAL
VOICES   Listening.

NANCY   Listening is also important when you are asking each other questions about the story. Let's think about questions for a moment. What is the difference between a question like "What color is Abbie's dress?" and a question like "In what ways did Abbie help her family?"

JENNY   The first one is easy. You don't have to think.

NANCY   So you need to ask questions that will make your partner think—really important questions.
    We've talked about the responsibilities we have with our partner to share the reading, to listen to each other, and to ask each other important questions. Your partner will be depending on you to do those things.

The children moved off in pairs to read the story together and then to ask each other questions about it.

CODY	Why was Abbie scared?
CHARLEY	She thought her papa might not come back.
CODY	And because she might not be able to light the lights, I think.

—

| BETH | Why did Abbie's father leave? Why couldn't they get a boat to bring them the things? |
| CHRIS | Yeah. |

—

STACEY	How do you think Abbie felt when her father left?
RICKY	Scared. But she went to see her hens and then she felt better.
STACEY	Why?
RICKY	Because they were her friends. Friends can help you when you feel bad.

SOME POINTS TO CONSIDER

✔ Nancy used the book *Keep the Lights Burning, Abbie* to highlight values her own students were practicing daily. While the literature made dramatic points about why dependability and responsibility are important qualities, Nancy focused on helping the children see themselves as responsible and dependable—in their daily lives as learning partners.

✔ The kinds of questions that Nancy encouraged her students to ask about the text are the kinds of questions that will help them in the future—as they try to solve problems, make choices, and understand a range of motivations for human behavior. "How do you think Abbie felt when her father left?" is not simply a question about Abbie and this particular book.

 Don't You Do What Your Dad Says?

Characters in literature don't have to exemplify values in order to make powerful points about values. Good literature typically takes the reader inside the doubts and tensions of trying to do the right thing, allowing the reader to consider and solve problems along with the characters. Literature that helps children recognize how complicated life is helps prepare them for that very fact.

When they discussed the complex decisions characters are faced with in the story "The Friendship," the fourth-graders in Brenda Henderson's classroom took into consideration the particular conditions (rural Mississippi, 1933) facing two would-be friends (an African-American boy named Stacey and a white boy named Jeremy); then they applied an overlay of their own experiences of what gets you in trouble with your parents and what ideas might be worth standing up for.

The teacher moved quietly around the room as children in partnerships discussed the challenges that would face Stacey and Jeremy if they decided to pursue their tentative friendship. We briefly visit three of these conversations.* (Because students are discussing issues of racial prejudice, their race is identified.)

A white girl and an African-American boy sat on the floor, backs against a wall.

BROOK   Do you think they could become friends?

JAMES   I think they could become friends.

BROOK   And that's why . . .

JAMES   But they'll certainly keep their own distance because if they didn't they could certainly get into a lot of trouble.

BROOK   I think that they could and they couldn't. They could because if they keep their distance, like you said, and if they're nice to each other and keep their friendship secret, they could be friends. But they couldn't because they have differences and during the time there will be a lot of pressure on them.

JAMES   I have one thing to say. Like, they can still have this friendship, but if they're still around each other as they get older, then they must keep the friendship. It won't be like Mr. Tom Bee and John Wallace's friendship. *[This interracial friendship was destroyed by the white man's cowardice in the face of pressure from his white peers.]*

BROOK   Yeah, like they learned their lesson from it.

A threesome "partnership" of two white girls and a white boy sat on desk chairs facing each other. The boy and one of the girls struggled with the friendship question.

PAUL   If I was Jeremy, I'd listen to my dad. Like, if my dad says, "Black people are bad, you shouldn't talk to black people," I wouldn't talk to them. I'd be like, "Shut up, get out of here, I don't like you, now leave."

---

* Excerpted from DSC Video Library, "A Friendship?"

JENNIFER   I wouldn't do that because a lot of people are just the same as anybody else.

PAUL   Well, do you listen to your dad?

JENNIFER   Well, I have to.

PAUL   Yeah, yeah! See, like if you listen to your dad now, you probably listened to your dad back then, 'cause, like, it's the thing you have to do.

An African-American girl and a white boy faced each other across a single desk. The boy was writing while the girl wavered about whether the two boys in the story should be friends.

NINA   I think . . . I think so . . . but if Jeremy thinks he shouldn't be friends because, because maybe the parents might get mad at him for being . . . like Stacey's parents would get mad at him for being with a white person and Jeremy's parents will get mad at him for being with a black person and get in trouble or something like that.

CORY   *(Nods)*

SOME POINTS TO CONSIDER

✔ In selecting this complex story for students to read, Brenda credits her students as thoughtful human beings. At the same time, she didn't start the year with this particular story. It is February and students have had many experiences of themselves as members of a caring community. They have also had many previous whole-class and small-group discussions about pivotal questions raised in literature (and life).

✔ Because Brenda visited with the various partnerships, she will be able to extend students' thinking with a whole-class discussion that incorporates their different concerns, such as whether young people can recognize and learn from bad examples—even when the examples conform to community or parental expectations. When Brenda continues the conversation with the whole class, it will be with everyone's voice and her own more expert facilitation.

✔ At the same time that teachers like Brenda seize opportunities to extend students' thinking, they also recognize that students need time on their own to consider and mull over big ideas; every discussion does not have to resolve itself with agreement or a definitive pronouncement.

■

As we have seen in this chapter, the teaching of humane values occurs in a rich range of ways—from setting class norms, to collaborative learning, to highlighting values in literature, and in all the hundreds of spontaneous interactions that make up a classroom day.

And because children quickly pick up the "messages" reflected in our delivery and language, in what we highlight and show that we like, our challenge is to make sure that our actions are congruent with our values. Children very quickly learn, for example, whether we actually value compliance over independent thinking, whether we truly respect each child in the classroom, and whether we can recognize fairness when it is ourselves who may have been unfair.

In the next chapter we will consider how children's experience of what we've called here "humane" values affects their intrinsic motivation to learn and to participate in the classroom community. The relationship, we will see, is a strong one.

Honoring Intrinsic Motivation

W HAT MAKES CHILDREN WANT TO LEARN? What makes them want to be caring and responsible? In every classroom children make choices about how to behave and what or whether to learn. Classroom environment goes a long way in determining what choices children will make about their behavior and learning; if we establish communities in which children feel included and valued, the choices children make will take teachers' concerns as well as their own into account. The overlap will be huge.

It's in There: The Biological Drives to Figure Out and to Fit In

A S TEACHERS, we can try to control children with extrinsic motivators, such as stickers, gold stars, blue ribbons, demerits, names on the board, and Fs. On the other hand, we can prepare children to control themselves by tapping into their intrinsic motivation to learn and to fit in. Because children are hard-wired to be curious and to be part of a social group, biology is a powerful ally when we try to help children develop responsibility for their own behavior and learning. Our challenge is to capitalize on these biological drives, not undermine them.

Children's intrinsic motivation to figure out and to fit in is not, however, a guarantee that they will want to learn what we are charged with helping them learn, nor that they will want to fit into the classroom community we have designed. It's hard to reach every child. Sometimes the community is perhaps too narrowly conceived and needs to be broadened to help children fit in. Sometimes we need to have faith in the research on children's resiliency, which finds that 50 to 75 percent of the children with the toughest life circumstances will overcome them if they have the support of just one adult. Giving up on children whose intrinsic motivation seems to be lost is to deny their biology—it's in there.

If we want to establish a caring learning environment that fosters and depends on children's intrinsic motivation rather than our external coercion, what strategies help?

Children's sense of themselves as members of a learning community is palpable in Marcia Davis's classroom.

Relevance: Connecting to Children's Lives

WHEN WE CONNECT school learning activities to children's concrete experiences of the world, we are tapping into their intrinsic motivation to figure out that world. As children pursue learning activities that are personally relevant, it also becomes relevant to learn the skills and understandings that go along with the activities.

 **Where Is May 9?**

In the story below, Marcia Davis described an experience with her grade two-three class in which she first ignored but then capitalized on the principle of connecting learning activities to children's lives.

MARCIA   Yesterday I tried a ditto sheet. We had one on reading a calendar that had questions like, "What day of the week will it be one week after May 9th?" Nobody knew how to do it. Nobody wanted to do it! My children are not too shy about it when they don't want to do something. I was frustrated, and so were they.

Then I remembered that I had a whole stack of calendars someone had given me. I thought using the calendars might make it more inviting to do the questions that were on the ditto sheet. Well, the children still didn't want to find May 9—they wanted to find their birthdays. So we spent some time just going around the room getting everyone's birthday and writing it in. It was a real learning process because the children had to know the order of the months to find them on the calendar, they had to find the correct date, and they had to spell their classmates' names. They also learned how to identify what day of the week corresponded to each date and ended up really learning everything that the ditto was designed to teach.

There was even a place on the calendars for telephone numbers, and somebody said, "We could put those in! Do you have a phone book?" So we got the phone book and we looked up numbers and we put those in and we talked about alphabetical order in a phone book and how you use it. We ended up having a wonderful lesson.

SOME POINTS TO CONSIDER

✔ The lesson Marcia learned was not that kids hate ditto sheets and love calendars, but that kids love birthdays! In this case the calendars gave children a way to shape the learning activity to meet their interests, whereas the ditto sheet had restricted them to an arbitrary, abstract learning activity.

✔ Once Marcia let her students' questions and interests drive their learning, their interest perked up. Their intrinsic motivation to learn what they want to know and to master skills relevant to their world turned this into a rich learning experience.

Relevance: Connecting to Usefulness

SOMEWHERE AROUND the ages of seven or eight, children begin to think of themselves as preparing to lead adult lives—and they begin wanting to do things not just because they are interesting, enjoyable, or immediately useful, but because these things will be useful to them as adults. This offers a second way to tap students' intrinsic motivation to figure out their world: help them realize how what they are learning is broadly useful, either now or for the future.

 Mrs. Biscardi, Why Are We Learning This?

As adults, we rarely learn something for which we couldn't answer the question: Why am I learning this? Dawn Biscardi encourages her third-graders to ask themselves that same question—and by defining uses and purposes for the learning they do, her students recognize and take pride in what they are accomplishing.

> For example, as her students concluded a study of Mexico for which they did a lot of research, Dawn called the class together for the conversation below.
>
> DAWN In your research on Mexico you have been doing many, many things. But my question to you is: What have you learned? I would like you to close your eyes and think about some things you learned from doing all of this.

The room was still as children sat quietly with their eyes closed. After a minute or so Dawn continued.

DAWN   Sometimes when you are getting ready to have a conversation, it helps to
         think beforehand of something to share. So I would like you and your part-
         ner to share your ideas about my question for three or four minutes. As you
         do this, I'm going to be listening for people asking their partner what they
         learned and sharing what they learned. Remember to talk first and jot ideas
         down later—it will help if you just try to remember things first.

After some busy partner discussion and writing, the children shared with Dawn what
they felt they had learned. Dawn listed their ideas on an overhead transparency:

> ## WE LEARNED
>
> - to listen
> - how to write a good report
> - to gather information
> - interesting things about Mexico
> - not to play around
> - how to work with a partner
> - how to write a semantic map
> - to organize
> - to fix mistakes and make it better
> - that it's not easy
> - about revising -- you can't just make one
>   copy -- you have to go through things
> - to try your hardest
> - how to accept advice

DAWN   What I'd like you to decide with your partner now is why it was important
         to learn these things. Think about what these will help you do—how they
         can help you as learners in the future. Take a couple of minutes to share
         ideas, and then I'll ask each pair to share one thing with the rest of the class.

As pairs of children brought their ideas back to the whole class, Dawn again recorded
on an overhead transparency:

> ## WHAT I WILL BE ABLE TO DO
>
> - write stories
> - pass exams
> - be a teacher
> - know more things
> - work with people
> - go to college
> - be a reporter and learn about other countries for when you go on trips
> - get a job to help others
> - work as a team
> - become smarter
> - not be afraid of trying things that are hard

DAWN   Look at all the things you have learned! *(With a conspiratorial lilt)* I feel a chart coming on . . . .

CLASS   *(Knowing giggles)*

DAWN   I'm wondering if you'd like to share this list with your parents—the way we did with our "Successful Writers" chart?

CLASS   *(Agreement around the room)*

DAWN   You know, teachers ask students a lot of questions, but if you are to be successful as learners you need to ask questions of yourselves, too. There are two questions I'd like you to think about asking yourself when you're learning something. *(Pausing, Dawn writes on the board)*

- Why am I learning this?
- How will learning this help me?

My job is to help you learn, but you have a responsibility to help yourself learn, too. If I'm teaching something and you are not clear, you need to question, "Mrs. Biscardi, why are we learning this?" or "What is our goal here?" or "How will this be useful to us?"

A POINT TO CONSIDER

✔ To help her students learn the things she is responsible for teaching, Dawn taps into their intrinsic motivation to prepare themselves for the future. She knows that learning for future purposes will become increasingly important to children as they move up the grades, so she helps children see that working hard to make oneself competent is inherently satisfying, even in cases when acquiring *certain* skills and knowledge may not be.

 Life Is Not Compartmentalized

In a conversation with Joan, Dawn described how she communicates to students her faith in learning.

JOAN   You seem to want children to get inside the process of learning, to have an appreciation of how and why they are learning things.

DAWN   Children learn when they have some reality connected to what they learn—when it touches their lives. So I talk with children about how learning is a process that they are engaged in personally and how we all bring different things to that process, make different connections, and make sense of things—for now and for the future.

JOAN   I noticed quite a change in Gregory's level of engagement when you helped him make the connection that the research he was learning how to do for the Mexico study could help him find out more about horses in the future.

DAWN   Yes, his passion is horses. Gregory was new to our school this year, and when he arrived he said he hated school. But I've seen his attitude slowly change, and I've worked hard to help him find learning meaningful. If I can make an attitudinal change in a child, I believe I will have done more than any "lesson" I could teach.

JOAN   What do you think has influenced you to work in this way?

DAWN   Age, commitment, and a lot of joy from seeing children interacting with each other and making meaning. Through a life of hits and misses, I've come to realize that all our learning and skills are intermeshed—life is not compartmentalized!

A POINT TO CONSIDER

✔ As she shows in Gregory's case, Dawn knows enough about her students to help them see the relevance of what they are learning, both in terms of connections to their current interests and to how this learning will serve them in the future. By establishing that learning is interesting and useful, Dawn makes learning something that she and her whole classroom community value.

Relevance: What the Community Values

A THIRD PRINCIPLE of intrinsic motivation is also demonstrated in Dawn's classroom: Children want to learn the skills and acquire the knowledge that is valued by their community—by the people they care about and the people they admire. It goes back to their intrinsic motivation to figure out and fit in.

To tap into this vein of intrinsic motivation, teachers like Dawn make their classrooms learning communities, make sure parents understand and are involved in the learning community, and establish caring relationships with their students.

The relationships that teachers establish with students, it should be understood, are not used to manipulate them. For example, Dawn does not make her caring relationship contingent upon her students' learning performance. Quite the reverse. Dawn cares unconditionally for her students. But she lets them know what she thinks is important for them to know, why it is important, and why she values kindness, hard work, responsibility, respect, and much more.

Because her students like and admire Dawn, they want to live by the values she holds up for them and to learn what she believes is important for them to learn—not to earn her favor, but because they trust and want to be like her.

Thinking about the parallels in our adult lives can clarify why a teacher's caring relationship with a child is a support for the child's intrinsic motivation, not an extrinsic motivator to bestow or withdraw. For example, sometimes we start a book and after a chapter or two decide it isn't worth finishing, only to take it up again when a trusted friend or mentor assures us that if we persevere we will find it worth the effort. We don't do this because we want to please our friend (an extrinsic motive), but because we trust that we will indeed find something of value in the book (an intrinsic motive). Just as trusted friends and mentors affect our adult attitudes and values, the classroom community and teachers' relationships with their students affect children's attitudes and values.

When children are in a caring community—that is, a community in which their basic psychological needs for autonomy, belonging, and competence are met—they want to live up to the community's values for learning and behavior.

 **No Outcasts**

But what about children who have not experienced school as a caring community or who have not experienced truly caring relationships before coming to school?

For many reasons, some children have not had their basic psychological needs for autonomy, belonging, and competence met in a school setting. Perhaps the gulf between their home culture and their school's culture is vast, perhaps they are not proficient in the skills valued by the school environment, or perhaps they are just different from their classmates in some particular way—for example, very overweight, very shy, a different race, or a different class. We can begin helping such children by modeling how to include them and by helping all students see each other's humanity and special attributes.

Still other children may be among the small percentage who have no adult at home who cares about them. Usually such children lack basic trust. They may segregate themselves from the classroom community through angry, selfish behavior—learned because they have always had to fend for themselves—or they may be incredibly demanding of their teacher's attention, never believing that they are safe unless they are being attended to. Establishing a trusting relationship with such children is a necessary and difficult first step in meeting their basic psychological needs (sometimes this requires assistance from a school psychologist or social worker). Finding ways to meet the needs of these children, something we would strive to do in any case, is also the way to foster their desire to be part of the classroom community and live by its values.

The teacher's role in trying to find ways to meet a particular child's needs includes modeling a "no outcasts" norm for the class. As Laura Ecken related below, it's not always easy to recognize the things you are doing that might be undermining the students' sense of community—but once you do recognize them, she pointed out, there's no turning back.

LAURA   Before I began to realize how important community was to kids' learning, I might have had twenty kids talking in my classroom but I would only write one kid's name on the board. It was a nice, easy way for me to shut the whole class up when I needed to do something. It was never my intention to humiliate a child, but in effect, that is what I was doing.

Laura Ecken sets a powerful example for her students by the respect she affords every child in the room.

When a child wouldn't come to the rug, I would put their name up on the board and fuss at them. I was causing that child to be an outcast. The other children were taking their lead from me. To myself I was thinking—this sounds horrible—"nobody likes that child." But I was setting it up. I just wanted to control the class. I just wanted to dismiss the child who wouldn't be part of the class. Basically I was saying, for everyone to hear, "You're not part of the class."

As I look back on it, the kids that got made fun of in the cafeteria or in line, the kids everyone refused to play with on the playground, were the kids I wasn't letting participate because they didn't know how to act.

We don't have those kinds of outcasts now. We don't have kids who are picked on that way. I have kids in my class who don't smell good, who wear shabby clothes, who don't really look good. But I don't have outcasts. The kids who might have been outcasts before are learning how to act, how to take responsibility.

I have one child, Mark, who every time I talked would pick up a table and drop it. In the past I would have put his name on the board but now I talk with him. This has really helped people accept Mark. Before, he would have been an outcast in a big way because I couldn't control him. And he didn't begin to control himself until January. There were months of my talking privately with him and asking questions—"What's the problem when you drop the table?" or "How's that affecting other people when you do that?" As the teacher, you have to keep at it.

SOME POINTS TO CONSIDER

✔ Helping Mark learn self-control skills was a proactive response, in contrast to Laura's earlier reactive response of putting student names on the board—and creating outcasts in the process.

✔ It took four months, but Laura's patient response helped Mark join the community and deterred his classmates from shunning him.

✔ In so many situations when children misbehave, it's not that they don't want to fit in, it's that they *don't know how*. Often the required behavior—paying attention, sharing, or refraining from teasing, insulting, or hitting others—seems to us obviously right and easy to do. But many children have not had the time or experience to see the world as clearly. If we respond to their inappropriate behavior by assuming a lack of knowledge, skills, or self-control, and if we then proceed to help children develop what they need to be successful, the offending behavior usually diminishes. And each time we help children succeed in doing the right thing, they are more likely to see themselves as someone who *can* succeed and to try even harder to do so in the future.

What Gets in the Way of Intrinsic Motivation?

T HE CONDITIONS DESCRIBED above—making connections to children's lives, to what will be useful to them, and to what the community values—enable us to tap students' intrinsic motivation to learn and to do the right thing. Failing to provide these conditions—or defaulting to their antitheses—will have correspondingly negative effects. So for example, when faced with a task that seems arbitrary because it has no connection to their lives or to their futures, children have little intrinsic motivation to master the task or the skills involved. Likewise, children who feel excluded from their classroom community may well reject that community's values.

In addition, three other conditions can get in the way of students' intrinsic motivation: failure to provide learning tasks with an appropriate level of challenge, overcontrolling a task, and using extrinsic motivators—including competition.

Too Easy — Too Hard

We can't possibly customize every activity for every student, but we know how important it is for an activity not to be either too hard for some or too easy for others.

If a task is too difficult—if children try and try and still fail—they will come to devalue the activity and stop trying. Success in return for effort is very motivating; but repeated failure in return for effort is deadly. Similarly, if a task is too easy, it holds nothing for children to figure out. Now and then it may be comforting for children to experience complete ease and confidence in completing a task, but as a steady diet, such "success" is empty and boring.

This is why it is so important to involve children in flexible learning activities in which they "customize" the lesson for themselves—participating at their own level of competence and learning what is next on their own developmental agenda. This means structuring not only open-ended activities, but also activities that allow children to try out, practice, experiment with, or perfect a variety of skills and abilities. Such activities can be as simple as letting children choose their own book for independent reading and their own way to share it with the class, or as encompassing as a whole-class integrated unit of study such as "Life in a Pond," described on page 95.

Like the activities we provide, the feedback and encouragement we give children are most motivating when addressed to their individual needs and competencies, recognizing how each child is growing.

A POINT TO CONSIDER

✔ Flexible, open-ended learning activities allow children's intrinsic motivation to flourish. Children are able to enter such an activity at their current level of competence, move in directions that have meaning for them, and receive feedback that develops and supports their skills and goals.

 ## I'm Going to Give You Ten Minutes

If children are to learn to take increasing responsibility for their learning and behavior, then their learning goals, activities, and processes mustn't be too tightly controlled. When every decision is made for them, when they have no voice in or ownership of their learning, children can feel they are just being "made" to do things and feel correspondingly resentful. And when children's role in the classroom is merely to follow directions, their investment in learning and in monitoring their own behavior suffers.

Like many points made in this book, we can appreciate the damaging effects of overcontrolling children if we think about parallel experiences in our adult lives. In the conversation below, Marcia Davis and Laura Ecken described a telling incident at a workshop they attended.

LAURA   When we were at a staff development workshop last summer, for the first time I really noticed how important the way you set up a learning activity can be. Some of the presenters, when they had something for us to do, would say, "I'm going to give you ten minutes to do this."

MARCIA   Oh, yes—*they* were going to "give us" ten minutes. It was so tempting to say, "You can have them back—we don't want them!"

LAURA   We felt put down. It was like they were in power and we were the little peons that they were telling what to do. It was like sitting there being part of a classroom. And I could imagine how the kids feel when they are dealt with that way. That was when I started to get really conscious of how I was running my own classroom and the language I was using that was speaking from a power position.

MARCIA   The hard thing was, we saw ourselves in that presenter. It is much easier to say to kids "I want you to . . ." or "I'm going to give you ten minutes" instead of "Let's take ten minutes and see how far we get with this," or even "How much time do you think we will need?"

LAURA   At least now I'm conscious of it—that's the first step.

A POINT TO CONSIDER

✔ Marcia and Laura recognize how demeaning it can feel to be on the receiving end of instructions that are addressed to you but fail to acknowledge that your engagement is important. For children as well as adults, when a task is overcontrolled, it is all too clearly an item on someone else's agenda.

 ## What's Going to Happen When the Rewards Run Out?

While overcontrolling the parameters of children's learning and behavior undermines their intrinsic motivation, at least it is overt. An indirect and more insidious method of controlling children is the use of extrinsic motivators—manipulating them with promises or threats, rewards or punishments, approval or withdrawal of approval.

Extrinsic motivators such as stickers, prizes, and punishments can certainly modify children's behavior for the short term, but their long-term effect is to focus children on the motivator—the prize or the punishment—rather than the learning or behavior. All students—those who get rewards and those who do not—learn less and are less committed to continued learning when they are motivated by extrinsic rewards rather than their own intrinsic motivation to figure out and fit in.

In schools that traditionally compare students with each other on a scale from A to F, it can be hard to break students as well as teachers from reliance on extrinsic motivators. Laura Havis describes how she helps students appreciate that no external standard should be higher or more meaningful than the standards they set for themselves.

JOAN   How do you communicate with your students about intrinsic versus extrinsic motivation?

LAURA   We start very early in the year and we talk about how we want our class to be. We talk about cooperation and what it means to be cooperative. And out of that conversation come ideas like: "When we cooperate everybody feels good about himself or herself." "We don't want to leave anybody out." "We're all part of a team, so for any of us to be successful we all must be successful."

As we work through it over time—and it has to be part of every single thing we do, not just a now-and-then thing—kids come to understand "This is the way we operate." It becomes internalized, a matter of course, a way of being.

JOAN   Where do you see extrinsic rewards fitting into this "way of being"?

LAURA   Philosophically, I don't. I feel very strongly about this. What's going to happen to the child when the rewards run out? When the kids ask me, "How did I do?" I say, "How do you think you did?" I give them feedback and I show them models with criteria for success, but I emphasize that they have to ask questions of themselves, like: "Did I do my best?" "Did I do as well as I think I could have done?" "What is it that I have done well?"

And the kids are learning to do that—they are learning to set high standards for themselves. And they're learning that if you value cooperation you compete against yourself rather than against others.

SOME POINTS TO CONSIDER

✔ Laura makes the most of children's intrinsic motivation by helping them understand that they each have a part to play in contributing to the whole, and that they can all work to be successful and support each other toward this.

✔ She doesn't resort to extrinsic motivators, but instead makes the criteria for success explicit, encourages students to set their own goals, and provides individualized feedback and acknowledgment to help learners understand and recognize their growing skills and competencies.

I Like the Way Kitty Is Sitting

No matter what we may believe about the power of intrinsic motivation and cooperation, many of us have been taught that competition is the most efficient way to promote learning. If we set children in competition against one another, this wisdom goes, they will learn because of their natural desire to be the best—to beat or outperform their classmates. And children *will* work to try to outperform their classmates—but at a very steep price both to their learning and to their relationships with each other.

When learning is the intended goal but competition is the motivator, children are quick to identify winning as the *true* goal. They focus not on learning, but on doing tasks faster or better than their classmates. And to increase their chances of winning, they are less likely to take the risks that lead to meaningful learning or that promote independent thinking or creativity.

Competition not only limits children's ability to learn, but it also limits their opportunities to feel successful. When winning is the goal, they can only feel successful when they win. The value of what they do and what they accomplish is entirely determined by others—those who set the task and those whom they beat. Accordingly, even the most "successful" children have a shaky sense of self-worth, since it remains high only as long as they continue to be the "best." As Australian educator Susan Hill has noted, "Being the best is a seductive concept, but it is a myth. No one can be the best forever."

And what about the children who don't win, especially those who *never* win? When winning is the gauge of success, all those who don't win are therefore "losers." What surer way to quash children's desire to learn than to lock them into competition that labels them "losers" time and again? Not only do such children become passive in a system that devalues them, but they are left with an even more tenuous sense of self-worth than their peers who win.

A particular form of competition that is not always recognized as such is a teacher's differential approval of some students and their behavior. A statement such as "I like the way Kitty is sitting so quietly and showing that she is ready to listen" causes students to see each other as competitors for our public approval. Those who win approval learn to disrespect those who don't, while the students denied approval learn to envy, dislike, and resent those who do.

Because this kind of competition leads to distrust and rancor, it denies children the benefits of positive peer relationships and undermines teachers' best efforts to build community. In fact, a competitive classroom makes it just about impossible to build a classroom community. When children must compete for limited prizes, grades, or approval, their classmates are their rivals, not their colleagues.*

---

*Nel Noddings, Professor of Child Education at Stanford University, writes extensively on caring school communities and has given a great deal of thought to whether competition has any place in a caring community. In *The Challenge to Care in Schools*, she suggests asking three questions to assess the appropriateness of a competitive activity: (1) Is it still fun? (2) Can you take at least some pleasure in the victory of your opponent? and (3) Does the competition result in a better performance or product? If the answer to all three is "yes," she does not consider that competitive activity damaging to a community or to the relationship between the competitors. See the Annotated Bibliography of Additional Resources on page 198 for additional information about Noddings's book.

SOME POINTS TO CONSIDER

✔ In addition to classifying children as "winners" and "losers," competition in a classroom deters children from defining their own success and their own reasons for learning.

✔ A teacher's differential approval can have the same undermining effect as more formal competition for grades or prizes.

✔ Competition creates rivals, not colleagues.

■

In this chapter we have seen not just how competition and other extrinsic motivators undermine intrinsic motivation, but how to capitalize on children's intrinsic motivation by connecting learning to what's relevant to them—their experiences, their future, and the values of their community. And we have seen the power of community to support children's development: When children feel a part of a caring community, they are intrinsically motivated to uphold its values for learning and behavior.

In the next chapter we will investigate how children make meaning and how teachers create learning opportunities that take into account six principles of learning.

Learning for Understanding

THINK OF A POWERFUL LEARNING EXPERIENCE. Chances are the learning was personally meaningful—it had connections to something you already knew or wanted to know. Chances are the experience was actively engaging—it got your mind or body moving. And chances are this learning experience helped you make better sense of the world or feel more competent managing your role in it. Such learning experiences are the ones children value as well, whether in or out of school, as they build and test their own rich theories about the world and try to master the competencies that give them choice and autonomy in navigating it.

Understanding Is ~~Hole~~ Whole

THERE ARE TWO common ways to think of learning. For behaviorists and "blank slate, empty vessel" proponents, learning is a storage process in which we passively accumulate new bits of knowledge and information. For constructivists and developmentalists, learning is an active process for building increasingly elaborate mental pictures or representations of what we "know," and connecting them with each other in increasingly complex ways. For constructivists, these mental pictures and their connections are stuff we work with, not stuff we store. These mental representations are continually subject to our tinkering, realignment, overhauling, retooling, and even abandonment.

An impressive body of research on cognition suggests that learning is, in fact, much more complex than can be explained with a storage model or achieved with rote learning of transmitted data or discrete skills. While some of the things we learn (for example, names, phone numbers, and musical scales) primarily involve remembering and require little or no understanding, most learning depends on understanding—otherwise we would be unable to develop, elaborate, or revise our mental representations of things and their *relationships* to other things.

From these *relationships* we build the frameworks, or theories, that allow us to order our world of facts, objects, people, places, events, and ideas. These relationships, by definition, make understanding whole.

Magnetic Shoes

What does the process of learning for understanding look like? How can a teacher promote it? Let's imagine the example of a young girl and her emerging understandings of Australia and gravity.

> A city child living in the United States—we'll call her Luanne—is sitting attentively in her kindergarten book circle. Her teacher—we'll call her Ms. Kay—reads the book *Farmer Schulz's Ducks* and shows children the pictures of the Schulz farm in the Australian countryside. The children discuss the story and ask questions.
>
> LUANNE   What is Australia?
>
> MS. KAY   Australia is a country that is far away.
>
> When Luanne hears this, what she understands about "Australia" is based on the connections she makes between the story and her existing knowledge. Luanne knows nothing about Australia, but she does know what "far away" and "country" mean.

LUANNE   *(Thinking to herself)* When we drove to Gram's farm in Iowa, it was far away. It was the country because there weren't even sidewalks.

Since Luanne has something she can connect Australia to, she automatically builds a mental picture of Australia as a country place like where her grandmother lives.

The following year, Luanne's class is learning about penguins. The teacher—we'll call him Mr. Jay—borrows a globe from the classroom next door to show children where penguins live. Australia is one of the places Mr. Jay points out.

LUANNE   Can we go to Australia to see the penguins?

MR. JAY   Australia is very, very far away. You can't even drive there. You have to fly in an airplane from the United States over the ocean *(Pointing on the globe)* and past all these countries like Japan and China. It takes so long that you have to sleep overnight right in your airplane seat. And then in the morning you still aren't there!

Luanne's concept of Australia becomes more accurate as she adjusts her earlier understanding to make sense of the new information. She now understands that Australia is not *in the country* like her grandmother's house, it is *a country*, different from other countries like Japan and the United States, and much farther away than Iowa (whatever that is). However, as Luanne reconstructs her mental representation of Australia, she also incorporates her experience with things that are "underneath," as Australia clearly is on the globe.

LUANNE   *(Musing to herself)* Why don't people in Australia fall off the world? There is nothing but air below them.

Later, as she is playing with her magnetic letters, Luanne realizes that they stick even when she holds the magnetic board upside down. She makes a new connection and tries out a more coherent and elaborate concept of Australia.

LUANNE   People in Australia don't fall off because they have magnets in their shoes.

A few days later Mr. Jay overhears Luanne describing to another student the magnetic shoes that people in Australia all wear.

MR. JAY   Tell me more about your idea, Luanne.

LUANNE   They have to wear magnets in their shoes or they would fall off the bottom of the world. The magnets hold them on.

Mr. Jay realizes that Luanne has constructed a theory to explain what she could not otherwise understand—people sticking to the bottom of the earth. Mr. Jay tries to help her think more clearly about Australia by presenting a challenge to Luanne's theory.

MR. JAY   What about the penguins?

LUANNE   Magnetic feet?

Mr. Jay realizes that he needs to present a more difficult challenge, something that will be harder for Luanne to fit into her theory. He finds a *National Geographic* that has photographs of people walking barefoot on an Australian beach.

MR. JAY   These people are on vacation in Australia. They came from the United States. Do people in the United States have magnetic feet?

LUANNE   *(Looking at her feet)* No.

MR. JAY   So why don't these people from the United States fall off the world when they go to Australia?

Luanne is stumped, so Mr. Jay explains that it's not magnetism that keeps people attached to Australia, but a different force.

MR. JAY   Gravity. Gravity is different from magnetism, but it is like magnetism in some ways. Gravity keeps *everything* on the world. All the people in the United States, all the people in Australia, all the animals, all the cars, the oceans, magnets!

Luanne abandons her theories of magnetic shoes and magnetic feet, which cleans up her understanding of Australia somewhat. But now she has a new concept—gravity—to try to understand.

LUANNE   *(Once again thinking to herself)* It must be a giant magnet . . . bigger than the Sears Tower.

SOME POINTS TO CONSIDER

✔ The process Luanne and all of us go through of building and refining our mental representations—based on experiencing the world, striving for coherence, making predictions, and making adjustments based on discrepancies between our predictions and reality—this process can be defined as learning for understanding.

✔ While people take in information in different ways, depending on what connectors the information strikes (for example, not every child in Luanne's class has a grandmother in rural Iowa, and not every teacher has sat in an airplane seat around the clock to Australia), the process of constructing and refining understanding holds true whether we are five or forty-five, whether we are a first-grader or a teacher, whether we think gravity *is* a magnet or is *like* a magnet (somehow).

Classrooms = Safe Places to Make Mistakes

If our goal is to help children learn for understanding, what kind of learning environment do they need? Two conditions—support and challenge—must be present.*

A supportive learning environment is one that supports children in building their own understandings or mental representations—in thinking for themselves and recognizing that their ideas and solutions may differ from those of others. When Luanne's teacher overheard her description of magnetic shoes, he didn't laugh at her or dismiss her thinking with a label like "cute." He asked for more information; he took Luanne's statement as evidence of theory-building.

Because children's representations are by virtue of their "childness" naive and incomplete, children require a learning environment that helps them confront discrepancies in their naive theories and build more coherent theories and mental representations. Mr. Jay challenged Luanne's magnet theories and introduced gravity as a concept for Luanne to be curious about.

Gradually, as her abstract reasoning skills develop, and *if* Luanne's teachers provide the time for her to ask questions, experiment, ask more questions, and confront discrepancies, her mental representation of gravity will become more accurate. By the time she encounters Newton's laws of motion and theory of gravity, Luanne will be ready to do the final concept building required to replace any traces of her magnet theory with this more coherent one.

The kind of time invested in getting Luanne to this point is no small matter amid the pressures of an ever-expanding curriculum and assessment systems that measure remembering rather than understanding. On the other hand, if Luanne's teachers focus primarily on telling her things to remember rather than supporting and challenging her to develop understanding, her theory about magnetic gravity, among others, will endure—in combination with an incompatible set of memorized but not understood facts, formulas, concepts, and theories.

Naive theories are powerful, and in the absence of coherent replacements, they persist. Some naive theories limit our understanding of the physical world—theories, for example,

* The work of cognitive psychologists Irving Sigel and Howard Gardner informs this discussion (and is reported in Motivation and Learning Theory: An Overview on pages 166–169).

about the sun going around the earth, or objects being solid. Some naive theories limit our understanding of the social world—theories, for example, about people who look different being untrustworthy, or people who don't speak our language being stupid.

Learning for understanding requires time and the courage to insist on it. Otherwise, for many children the lack of coherence between their naive theories and what they are taught makes it too hard to learn and, therefore, too hard to care about learning. And when naive social theories persist, it's not just the learner who is harmed.

SOME POINTS TO CONSIDER

✔ We support children's learning by taking their theory-building seriously, maintaining a classroom community where students take each other's ideas and efforts seriously, and providing time for children to explore their ideas.

✔ We challenge children's learning by helping them ask questions and recognize discrepancies in their mental representations and theories.

Six Significant Principles of Learning

A WHOLE HOST of principles related to good learning are reflected in many different settings throughout this book. Our intention here, though, is to focus on those principles most central to helping children learn for understanding. The questions below apply to any learning environment.

1. *Content: Is it important?*
   Is the curriculum focused on important questions that children (and all human beings) want to know about—questions about themselves and how they differ from others; about society and the social/moral world; about the biological world and the physical world that surrounds them?

2. *Context: Is there one?*
   Are children *using* important processes and learning skills instead of just *practicing* them for their own sake? For example, are reading, writing, listening, computing, categorizing, and remembering taking place in the service of understanding—in a context that matters to the learners?

Because Terry Rice's sixth-graders regularly work in collaborative groups, they have lots of opportunities to build the trusting relationships that allow them to challenge as well as support each other.

3. *Connections: Are children helped to see relationships?*
   Do questions and the design of the learning environment encourage children to see new relationships? Is children's understanding being scaffolded, supported, or nudged by connecting new learning to children's lives, past experiences, and current understandings?

4. *Processes: Do they promote understanding?*
   Do children have lots of opportunities to engage in active processes such as discovery, observation and description, collaborative dialogue, prediction, and formulation of and inquiry about their own questions?

5. *Representations: Do children have multiple ways to represent their thinking?*
   Are children encouraged to build their representational competence by expressing their thinking in multiple ways—for example, in writing, pictures, graphs, diagrams, and drama?

6. *Community: Does it support and challenge understanding?*
   Do children feel encouraged to figure out and safe enough to make mistakes? Are children helped to see discrepancies in their thinking?

These principles are not new or unique. They are reflected in a wide variety of education-al policy and curriculum reform documents because they are congruent with what is known about how people learn.

 ## She Broke the Law for a Good Cause

What does it look like when we put these six principles into practice? The students in Becky O'Bryan's grade four-five classroom know. They experienced the whole set of them one morning—when a partner discussion after a teacher read-aloud moved into small-group Venn diagramming, then partner dialogue-writing, then classroom conversation.*

A Question Is Introduced

Becky concluded reading aloud to students a chapter from a biography, *Freedom Train: The Story of Harriet Tubman.*

BECKY   "As a conductor of the Underground Railroad, I can say what most conduc-tors can't," she grinned. "I never ran my train off the track, and I never lost a passenger."

Becky closed the book and gave students time to absorb this latest chapter describing Harriet Tubman's lifelong quest to free individual slaves and end the practice of slav-ery in the United States. Becky then drew students' attention to a focus question she had written on the blackboard.

BECKY   I've got up here a statement:

> *Harriet was single-minded about her work as a conductor on the*
> *Underground Railroad. What do you think about the fact that she*
> *broke the law, that she stole, lied, drugged crying babies, and threatened*
> *fearful runaways with a gun in the back to move on?*

Talk about this issue with your partner, then turn to the people across from you and continue talking in a foursome.

The children had strong feelings and opinions, both about Harriet Tubman and the issues she represented. In the three groups below, students explored the idea of civil disobedience and the obligation to obey a "higher" law.

* Excerpted from DSC Video Library, "Harriet Tubman and Tim Meeker."

ARETHA   I think she wasn't gonna kill 'em or anything. I think she knew what she was doing.

BARRY   Yeah, I agree. She broke the law for a good cause 'cause it shouldn't be right to have one person own another person.

ARETHA   I think so, too. Like when she stole—she did everything for a cause, really.

——

IZZY   She broke the law first of all by going against her slave owners.

JACKIE   But she was helping us get to where we are by breaking the law.

KENT   By breaking a small law, she was trying to keep a big law.

——

ELIZA   I think that she did the right thing.

CALVIN   By breaking the law?

ELIZA   Yeah, I think so.

CALVIN   Why?

ELIZA   Well, I would have done it if I was brave enough. I mean, it was wrong to hold on to them slaves.

In another group, children explored the nature of racism and the question of whether the Civil War really did free the slaves.

DARRELL   It's kind of weird, though. First there was the Civil War—it was like the century before the civil rights movement—and you're right, blacks really weren't free until the civil rights movement. Until this day there's racism, and probably centuries beyond there will be.

LINDA   Is there any way of really stopping racism?

DARRELL   But there's racism all over. People hate Germans, and they hate Chinese, they hate Asians. People hate white and black.

LINDA   It's not just white against black and it's not black against white. It's all around, you know. It's different cultures against different cultures.

Becky moved quietly among groups, mostly listening. Sitting in on one group's conversation, she described a connection that occurred to her between what they were discussing and the Holocaust. One of the students in the group suddenly made another connection.

ARETHA   This kind of reminds me of *The Ten Commandments* on TV last night, too, because the people were following Moses to freedom—the slaves in Egypt were following Moses to freedom. And some of the people didn't believe, didn't have faith to go on. And some of the people that she [Harriet] was going to hurt with the gun didn't have faith to go on either.

Students Investigate Two Characters

Following the small-group conversations, Becky brought the class back together and asked them to step back in their minds to January, when they had read about Tim Meeker's experience during the Revolutionary War in the novel *My Brother Sam Is Dead.* Becky asked children to work in the same groups of four to create a Venn diagram comparing Harriet and Tim. Ideas from three of the groups are recorded below.

AMY   They both matured in a different way. Tim matured when he had to take the wagon back. And, you know, it was scary. And so did Harriet—

JESSICA   Having to escape for the first time.

AMY   Yeah, she matured that way. So they were both—they both matured scaredly, or something like that. *(She chuckles at the word she creates to convey her meaning)*

DAVID   Well, I think that Tim—well, he had two people in his family die, and Harriet said none of her slaves have ever died and she'd be more careful, but Tim is—

JESSICA   She's more, like, *responsible*.

DAVID   Yeah, and Tim had somebody in his family die and had that experience.

SUSAN   *(Thoughtfully)* She's not more *responsible*. It's just that she's made more people escape—

AMY   She's *had* more responsibility to do than Tim. Tim hasn't had a lot of responsibility.

DAVID   Yeah, and Tim can't get beat up with a whip or nothing, but Harriet, whenever—

JESSICA   He was kind of safer than Harriet.

    —

TIFFANY   Tim coulda went off just like his brother did—

XAVIER   *(Cutting Tiffany off)* But it's not about—

TIFFANY   *(Cutting Xavier off)* I know! But they keep fighting the wars!

VAN   *(To Tiffany)* Well, look, tell us what you were going to say.

TIFFANY They both gave up something they loved. Tim had to give up his father and his brother to the war, and Harriet had to give up her parents.

———

IZZY   Tim was confused about the war.

OWEN   Harriet knew exactly what side she was on and Tim didn't know.

IZZY   They both had to deal with death.

As groups finished their Venn diagrams, Becky introduced the next topic: What might Tim Meeker and Harriet Tubman say to each other if they met? (Tim had expressed grave doubts about the value of war to settle conflict.)

Returning to their original partnerships, children negotiated the perspective each would take and developed and wrote an imaginary dialogue between Harriet and Tim. Partners then role-played these for the class. Three of the role-plays are recorded below.

HARRIET If it takes a war to free the slaves, I will be willing to fight myself. My dream is to free the people.

TIM   I understand your reasons, but still, why not try to talk about it, or have you already tried that? But I had a family member in the war. What about that situation?

HARRIET Talk! . . . I would if I could but white people just won't listen. I'm sorry, but you people are so pig-headed. Well, not all of you, only slave owners. I have not tried it [just talking] but I couldn't if I wanted to.

———

HARRIET War hurts. I know it does. But sometimes it is needed. Everyone is free now because of the war. I was sorry for all the casualties of the Civil War, too. It had to come sometime.

TIM   How come it had to come sometime?

HARRIET Some people's minds were set on fighting and they would get what they wanted no matter what. Only *they* could stop themselves.

TIM   War didn't have to come exactly at that time. I know it's not coincidence but war could have waited out at least mine, my brother's, and my father's life.

———

TIM   I think that there are more civilized ways to solve the problem. What do you think?

HARRIET Well, I think that war may never be necessary, and slavery ain't right either. You got a point. What do you think about slavery?

TIM   I think slavery is very, very wrong. The only reason why it doesn't say that in the Bible is because God thought people would have enough common sense to know it's wrong.

Students Investigate Their Own Opinions

Having overheard confusion in a number of partnerships about what qualifies as a "war," Becky invited a class discussion about it, which then became an impassioned exchange of opinions about the role of war—a discussion that was so important to students that Becky had to intervene to get them to go to lunch.

JENNIFER [Before the Civil War began] even though they did have laws, they was always fighting against the laws. So to me they were still fighting even though they had not fired the first hit.

ELIZA   Like the slaves and masters were. I think it was sort of like a war going on between them.

DAVID   It's like the master would always win, because all he had to do was get a whip and he would start hitting them with a whip or something. The only thing the slave would be able to do to win was just run away. And that was the same way with Tim. Like, he couldn't change the people's mind of killing his brother, because like, the Colonel said, "No, he's going to be killed." They wanted to set an example of him.

JESSICA Well, with the slaves and stuff, I think that even before guns were involved they were still fighting because a lot of times words can hurt more than a gunshot 'cause they were fighting with words a long time before the war.

CALVIN   Like a cold war.

BECKY   What do you mean?

CALVIN   You're really having a war, but you're talking, like. If you and somebody else was in, like, a debate or something, you'd still be fighting a war because you'd be going against each other. But you're just talking, not fighting using guns or materials.

TIFFANY The war didn't have to come. It could have been solved another way. These kinds of problem could have been talked about. And if you look back on these wars, maybe in the future when there's a problem like this you don't have to have war, you can talk it out.

JENNIFER   Maybe they didn't have to have a war, but at some point I think they did because on the point of the slaves—because that had gone on for so long and they had tried, they had tried to get it out, but it just seemed that they wouldn't. They kept on pushing and something had to give. On that point I do think there was a war needed.

TIFFANY   But no one really gained anything out of the war. There may not be slavery now because they had a war, but, Jennifer, if you really look at it, it could have been solved in another way besides war. Look at how many people were lost in every war.

SOME POINTS TO CONSIDER

Let's highlight specific ways the six principles played out in this classroom.

✔ *Content: Is it important?* The content evoked by the initial question about whether Harriet Tubman was right to break the law was immediately important to students because it forced them to reconcile their growing admiration for her with their legalistic notions of right and wrong.

Additionally, because students read accounts of war by a fictional character their age and as experienced by a historical figure they admired, the experience of war and its causes became real and relevant to them. Their effort to understand war became an effort to understand human nature—a matter of great personal importance to students.

✔ *Context: Is there one?* Students applied and practiced their growing communication skills of speaking, listening, reading, and writing, plus analytical skills of drawing on data to support arguments, making comparisons, taking different perspectives, and synthesizing information from different sources. All this was done within the context of answering questions and gaining understanding of things the students cared about.

✔ *Connections: Are children helped to see relationships?* Both formally and informally, Becky helped the students see relationships and make connections. She chose a focus question for children's first discussion that caused them to consider the relationship of political law and "higher" law. With the Venn diagram activity, she provided a structure that helped students see relationships between Harriet and Tim. And with the dialogue activity students were able to take what they had discovered about Harriet and Tim's relationships to another level, making connections between each character's experience and what that might lead each to say to each other. Informally, Becky made a connection between slavery and the Holocaust that helped Aretha make a connection between

Students in Becky O'Bryan's class have come to experience themselves as interesting, thoughtful human beings. They are in the habit of making connections between the lives they lead in and out of school.

Harriet and Moses. When Becky picked up that students had some big ideas about war and resolving conflict that they hadn't been able to articulate through the personas of Harriet and Tim, she made time for them to talk about their personal connections to these ideas.

✔ *Processes: Do they promote understanding?* In this example, peer conversation was a powerful process for scaffolding children's understanding. Group members repeatedly nudged each other into clearer or more elaborate understandings as they thought together about relationships between Harriet and Tim. Students also had an opportunity to formulate and explore their own questions—about whether war has to be "declared" and whether war is ever needed.

✔ *Representations: Do children have multiple ways to represent their thinking?* Becky's students represented their thinking in conversation, organized Harriet's and Tim's characteristics graphically in a Venn diagram, and wrote and dramatized dialogues for their classmates.

✔ *Community: Does it support and challenge understanding?* Becky's initial question presented a challenge to the students' conventional understanding that laws must always be obeyed. In their various discussions, the children provided challenge to each other by pondering together, disagreeing at times, and refining each other's ideas. Evidence of a supportive community included the absence of rancor and the fact that the children were willing to risk stating controversial opinions and to struggle jointly for understanding. Because time had been taken throughout the year to establish caring relationships, the children were able to engage in challenging conversation in a supportive and productive way.

 **Life in a Pond**

In Becky's classroom, we saw the learning benefits of a caring classroom community and got a sense of the interconnectedness, or wholeness, of the learning that goes on in that room. The sketch below is another demonstration of learning made whole for children, this time in two grade two-three classrooms where Marcia Davis and Laura Ecken co-planned major elements of a study of life in a pond.

A First Trip to Iroquois Park: Gathering Information and Questions

The children's study of life in a pond began not with a pond but with an oak tree. As Marcia finished reading aloud the story of the life cycle of a great oak, the children silently considered the tree's gradual return to the earth.

JONATHAN I've seen a tree like that in Iroquois Park. Could we go there?

Many voices joined Jonathan's, and Marcia and Laura could see that a visit to Iroquois Park would have many links to the work children had been doing in science. And so, an exploratory trip to the park was arranged, and children made a class web about what they might see and like to investigate.

The classes walked to the park together. In this visit, the focus was on discovering what was there. Learning partnerships observed and examined insects, animal homes, and trees. They looked for evidence of the decay and damage that cause all organic matter to return to the earth. They made notes and drawings, took photographs, and began asking themselves questions.

In a photographic class book, Bradley described a photo of himself and his partner making field notes:

> *Robert and I were working as partners and I was feeling something and telling him what it felt like and Robert was writing it and drawing it. I was feeling a stick. We took turns drawing and writing and feeling stuff.*

Marshelle's caption for a photograph of a tree demonstrated her understanding of insects' role in the life cycle of a tree:

> *It is bad to carve your initials on a tree because it will die. Nobody should carve their initials on a tree because the bugs will get into the tree. They would go through the bark to the inside of tree. The bark protects the tree.*

Antonio described a photograph of partnerships of students sitting with clipboards by the edge of the pond:

> *This is kids drawing pond animals. We had fun that day. We saw tadpoles. Tadpoles change into frogs. We have partners helping us.*

It became evident to Laura and Marcia that children were especially interested in the pond, so for the next several days students were given time to gather more pond-related information, books, and resource materials from the library and from home. They read individually and with their partners. Marcia and Laura read aloud to them. They reflected on their field experience in partnerships and as a class. They wrote in their journals about what they were learning.

Children's ideas and learnings were also reflected in the growing number of charts, diagrams, and webs displayed around the two rooms, some in the teacher's writing, some written by children. Children, for example, wrote and signed their questions about pond life:

> *How do turttlse cling to the pond?* K. G.
>
> *how Do the fish Die?* Chris
>
> *How many fish are there?* Andy

Making Curriculum Decisions: Building on Children's Interests

Laura and Marcia used their regular lunch meetings to co-plan around key concepts and understandings that they could see emerging, consciously looking for connections with the district science curriculum. They decided to focus on the following:

- All living things have certain characteristics in common, but they also have differences.
- No one living thing stands alone—all are connected to and depend upon many other things.
- Organisms live together in populations and communities.
- Each organism (or person) has an influence on the entire community.

Together, they looked at the kinds of experiences that would help children develop these understandings, and how this science unit could be integrated in meaningful, authentic ways with other curriculum areas. They also shared ideas about how to help children connect these understandings to an earlier social studies unit on Living and Working Together, in which they had focused on how each of their classrooms functions as a community.

Marcia and Laura brought the science teacher, Lynn-Earl Huddleston, into their planning, and agreed that in the science lab he would emphasize the scientific method (AKA "guess, test, report") with children.

Children's fascination with pond life suggested that a second visit to the pond would be valuable. Laura and Marcia negotiated with the children about some social goals for the trip and helped them transform their questions into specific learning goals. With these goals in mind, partners planned what to observe, how to record their observations, and what to collect for further study.

Children sat two by two around the edge of the pond, drawing and writing about what they were observing. Clipboards passed back and forth as partners commented on each other's work. Parent volunteers helped as children collected pond water, algae, and soil samples from the edge of the pond.

The next day children used their clipboard information to write in their journals all the things they had learned. They listed the things they had observed at the pond and created categories for them. Tim put his lists of "animals in the pond" and "animals out of the pond" into the diagram below.

In response to Laura's question "How can we re-create the pond to show what we have learned?" students agreed to make a giant mural. Then they discussed how to go about it so that they could end up with a whole picture of the pond—instead of twenty-eight snakes and no tadpoles, for example. Children reviewed the class norms on the bulletin board and agreed that the process needed to be fair for everyone. They decided to use the categories they had devised earlier as a way to divide the work among different groups. One group would do animals inside the pond, another group would do plants outside the pond, and so forth. Each group then negotiated internally as to who would make what and how they would share responsibility in a way that was fair.

The mural that emerged across the classroom walls captured a huge pond at work, with explanatory labels written by children. This strong visual record provided a stimulus for much writing, both scientific and creative. Laura also used the mural as a stimulus to have children think about and decide what they now wanted to learn more about.

Students formed interest-based partnerships, and Laura led a discussion about how to ensure that their new partnerships would get their research questions answered *and* honor the class norms.

While the research questions were different for different partnerships, Laura and Marcia wanted all children to improve their note-taking skills and their ability to draw out main points. They talked with children to help them understand the purpose and importance of being able to do this, both from the perspective of a "research scientist" and with regard to how this would be useful to children in their learning now and in the future.

Laura read children a short article about life in a pond and modeled the self-monitoring a good reader does, asking herself out loud, "Did that make sense? Should I read that again?" and "What is important for me to remember here?" Over the next few days, she read several short pieces, and children practiced telling a partner the important things to remember, then made notes that would help them remember the main points.

In the science lab, Lynn-Earl worked with each class of young scientists. In teams of three, children brainstormed what they thought might be contained in the samples they had brought back from the pond, then set up hypotheses that they shared with the class. The teams experimented with samples and examined them under a microscope, then recorded their conclusions in writing and drawing.

Children's discovery of paramecia in the pond water led to further discussion of systems and how things depend on each other. Laura helped children connect this in a personally meaningful way by asking them to think about "Who depends on me?"

Students' journal entries included the following:

My parents depend on me to do the dishes.

My pets depend on me to feed them.

Mrs. Ecken depends on me to listen.

My partner depends on me to be fair.

Children's growing understandings were reflected in other journal writings, as well.

The fish are like us because someday we will die and the fish will, too. We move around and the fish move around, too. We eat and the fish do, too. We're alive and the fish are, too. We're both animals.

The pond is like our classroom because the pond animals depend on each other for food and we depend on each other for helping. The pond is like us because we both live in peace. The pond has peaceful sounds like crickets and our class has peaceful music like Mozart.

"How could we assess our learning from this unit?" Marcia asked her students. Some children suggested writing, others drawing, and some decided to act out what they had learned. Following performances by two groups, the class reflected on drama as a way to demonstrate learning.

TIM   I think acting it out is a good way to show what you know. It's challenging to us to think up how to show it, and it's challenging to the audience because they have to watch us and pay attention and think about in the back of their heads what they know about ponds.

KRISTINA When they acted it out I could see what happens in ponds, like the big fish eat the little fish.

MARQUITA When I didn't know how to show that ponds are sometimes made by glaciers, Tim helped me.

MARCIA   These were certainly "successes." What about any "rough spots"?

ERICA   It's hard to do it with other people because everybody has to make up the characters and find out the best way. And you have to act out each person's way to find the best way. Then you have to practice. That takes a long time!

ANDY   Some of it was so funny we were falling down and acting goofy. It was fun, but we had to stop jumping around and pulling people down because we thought the kids would not be able to understand what we were acting if we acted goofy.

SOME POINTS TO CONSIDER

The principles central to learning for understanding were threaded throughout this unit of study, and many of the interwoven activities demonstrated more than one principle. For the purpose of illustrating the principles with concrete examples, however, we will ignore the "wholeness" of the learning experience and look at some of its discrete pieces.

✔ *Content: Is it important?* In following the children's interest in the pond at Iroquois Park, Marcia and Laura capitalized on children's inherent need to understand their physical and biological world. They know these are things children care about. They also recognized that they could plan the Life in a Pond unit with a focus on several key understandings from the district science framework. Throughout the unit, children were developing understandings of important concepts such as dependence and interdependence, how scientists work, and how partners and co-workers behave fairly and responsibly.

✔ *Context: Is there one?* Within the context set by children's interest and a set of key science understandings, the teachers helped children set personal learning goals and purposes—another kind of context. Nested in all of these contexts were children's use of processes and skills such as researching, drawing, writing, speaking, categorizing, and note-taking.

The work children did in partnerships and small groups provided yet another kind of context, one in which children practiced a range of social and problem-solving skills—from deciding who gets to carry the clipboard to agreeing how to organize the work of contributing to the class mural.

✔ *Connections: Are children helped to see relationships?* Laura and Marcia helped children connect their learning to what they already knew and what they wanted to know. Children were encouraged to make these kinds of connections from the moment Jonathan announced, "I've seen a tree like that in Iroquois Park."

Activities were structured to help children make connections between dependence in a biological community and dependence in a social community, see relationships between life in a pond and life in a classroom, and see relationships between their behavior and other people's learning—in partnerships and in the whole group. As Andy said in discussing "rough spots" in the group work, "We thought the kids would not be able to understand what we were acting if we acted goofy."

✔ *Processes: Do they promote understanding?* Children's visits to the park, their observations and experiments, their reading to answer their own questions, their reflections with partners and in their journals, their partner and group collaborations, their personal and group assessments of their learning—all contributed to children's understanding of important science content and helped them make significant connections to other learning and experiences.

✔ *Representations: Do children have multiple ways to represent their thinking?* Children recorded and represented their learnings and investigations in many different ways—through drawings, diagrams, webs, writing, photography, dialogue, drama, and murals.

✔ *Community: Does it support and challenge understanding?* Children were challenged continually—to make predictions about what they would find at Iroquois Park and in the samples they brought back, to negotiate learning and social goals for themselves and their groups, and to assess their own learning and behavior. They were supported by being treated as authentic learners and responsible members of the community, and that is how they responded.

■

In this chapter we have seen that knowledge of how children learn and how to facilitate that learning makes a teacher's job both more complex and more straightforward. Mastering these sophisticated understandings and leadership skills takes time and practice. Yet because teachers like Becky, Marcia, and Laura are clear about the principles of powerful learning, they can connect everything they do to their own big picture, or framework, of the key concepts, processes, and skills that are the basis for all important learning. When we work at building our own big picture of what good learning involves, and are clear about what is important for children to learn, we can connect everything we do to this and avoid the fragmented, additive model of learning that asks us to squeeze more and more of less and less importance into children's school experience.

The four keys to classroom community—fostering caring relationships, teaching humane values, honoring intrinsic motivation, and learning for understanding—provide a framework for creating a caring classroom where everyone learns. In the next section of this book, teachers share some practical tips for getting started with this kind of teaching and working through the rough spots.

Practical Tips from Teachers

THINKING BIG, STARTING SMALL

ROUGH SPOTS

GETTING COMFORTABLE

Thinking Big, Starting Small

E VEN WHEN WE ARE CLEAR ABOUT THE principles of powerful learning, including the role of caring relationships in a classroom community, it takes time to try out new ways of doing things, make "mistakes," reflect on and learn from those mistakes, and integrate new understandings into the core of our classroom management and teaching practices. In addition to our own learning journey, our students may have had little practice collaborating, taking responsibility for their own learning, or consciously trying to incorporate kind and respectful behavior into all their interactions. Sometimes, the idea of managing so many changes at once, for ourselves and our students, seems overwhelming. It usually helps to start such a journey one step at a time—thinking big, but starting small.

The Value of Familiar Formats

A MANAGEABLE STARTING place for many teachers, who either are themselves trying out new ways of organizing teaching and learning or have students whose prior learning experiences have been largely individualistic and unreflective, is with a collection of collaborative learning formats that become familiar over time.

These familiar formats, such as Interviewing or Group Poetry, stay constant even as the specific content changes. So, for example, partner interviews can be about many topics—ways to help, a treasured artifact, what was learned in a textbook chapter, what was learned from a parent in a home interview, or what makes us scared (see "If They Are Locked in the Bathroom . . ." on page 18, "You Brought It in a Bag . . ." on page 22, and "Kindergarten *Is* Cooperation" on page 52, for example). No matter what the interview topic, the familiar interviewing format provides that students will always share the talking time, will report or write or draw about their *partner's* information, not their own, and will always check with their partner first before sharing information from the interview.*

For children, familiar formats enable them to consciously focus—for a limited period of time—on working collaboratively and what this means. Such formats allow children to build their collaborative skills gradually, until these skills become natural and automatic.

For teachers, familiar formats let us focus more of our time on children's learning and interactions, and less time on handling logistics or questions about directions.

The Format of Formats

Formats for collaborative activities typically have three main parts: introduction, group work, and reflection. Within each of these parts, students encounter both academic and social learning.

Introduction	*Group work*	*Reflection*
Academic Learning	Academic Learning	Academic Learning
Social Learning	Social Learning	Social Learning

Designing a lesson using a collaborative format means starting, as usual, by deciding our purposes—but including social purposes or goals along with whatever academic ones we have chosen.

---

* Sample formats for Interviewing and Poetry are provided on pages 181–193 in the Resources section. A collection of 25 formats (including, for example, Mindmapping, Investigating, Editing, and Role-Plays) and about 200 activity suggestions appear in another Developmental Studies Center publication, *Blueprints for a Collaborative Classroom.*

TEACHER ROLE for group work	STUDENT ROLE for group work
1. Introduce the lesson to students	**1. Get ready to work**
Provide academic preparation	Learn about your job
• Make connections	• Focus your attention
to students' lives	• Look for connections
to future usefulness	*to your interests*
to community values	*to what you already know*
• Supply information (as needed)	Think about how you will do the task
content background	• Ask questions if you don't
modeling task processes	understand how or why you should
Provide social preparation	engage in the task
• Make connections	Think about how your group will work
to students' lives	together
to future usefulness	• How will you work fairly and
to community values	considerately?
• Supply information (as needed)	• How will you help your group
modeling collaborative behaviors	do its best work?
2. Observe student groups	**2. Work in your group**
Collect ideas for class reflection	Focus your attention and effort on
• Successes: academic and social	your learning
• Challenges: academic and social	• Be sure you understand what you
Ask questions of groups (as needed)	are doing and learning
• Get groups on track	Focus your attention and effort on how
• Focus students' thinking	you are interacting
• Deepen students' thinking	• Treat each other considerately
	• Share your ideas
	• Listen to the ideas of others
	• Make decisions fairly
3. Facilitate class reflection	**3. Reflect: How did it go?**
Facilitate discussion of academic	Think about what you learned or what you
learning and invite students to share	accomplished
products (as appropriate)	• Share your learning or
• Successes	accomplishments with classmates
• Challenges	• Listen to and learn from what your
Facilitate discussion of social learning	classmates share
• Successes	Think about your behavior and your group
• Challenges	interactions
	• Share your thoughts with classmates
	• Listen to and learn from what your
	classmates share

In the chart to the left we've expanded the three-part lesson format, showing the parallel roles for teachers and students and showing how to provide for both social and academic learning throughout.

In any given format, the student role labeled to the left as "2. Work in Your Group" is replaced with format-specific directions. For example, for a partner interview the teacher might provide directions such as the following:

Partner Interview Directions

1. One of you ask questions; one of you answer.
2. Switch roles.
3. Decide what to write/draw about your partner.
4. Check with your partner whether the information is okay to share.
5. Write/draw the information you chose and your partner said was okay.
6. Check with your partner whether your writing/drawing is accurate.
7. Fix anything that is inaccurate and check again.

Familiar three-part formats, including their predictable directions to students, allow students and teacher to focus on learning, not on activity steps and directions. Many of the teachers we visit in this book have found that having children collaborate within the bounds of a familiar format is a secure beginning for everyone toward the long-range goal of a more seamlessly collaborative classroom.

 **First We Talk**

First-grade teacher Karla Moore has found that familiar formats for collaborative activities help her because she can "get all the parts in, get the steps in place, and then extend the processes and carry them over to other activities."

> In the scene below, Karla's students recalled a poem about *The Twelve Sleeping Princesses* that they wrote in collaborative groups and prepared to use this same group poetry format to write a new poem based on their study of weather.

> KARLA   Let's remember some of the things we have done to learn about weather. Who has an idea?

JEROME   We made a cloud math book.

JACK   We started doing our weather calendars.

SARAH   We went outside and looked up at the clouds.

ANTHONY   You read us *[It Looked Like] Spilt Milk*.

ROSIE   We made a rainstorm with our hands and feet.

KARLA   Yes, today I want you to be remembering all those things about weather because we are going to be making a poem about it. Remember last week when we went to see *The Twelve Sleeping Princesses*, and we came back and made a poem with our partner?

          This time we will be making our poems about weather, and we will be making them on big posters so our parents can see what we have learned about weather.

Karla quickly sketched on the board the steps children would use to do this, numbering from 1 to 4. Children supplied the words to accompany the familiar pictures of talking heads, a light bulb, a pencil, and a marker.

SABRINA   First we talk.

KARLA   Yes, you talk to your partner about anything you want to say about weather.

JON   Then we each come up with an idea!

JAMES   Then we write it down about weather. In pencil first.

KEVIN   And then we copy over in marker.

Karla explained further that after partners write their sentences, they will get together in a group of four and put all four of their sentences into a poem.

KARLA   Now, I need a helper to come up here and be my sentence partner. Watch especially what we do that is kind.

After Karla and Johanna completed their role-play, children described what they noticed.

CHERYL   You were not looking at someone else.

JEROME   You were not interrupting.

SUSAN   You were telling her nice things.

SABRINA   She was talking to you.

DEBORAH She helped to figure out what to write.

Karla now called on Effrain to help her out, and she modeled the opposite of being kind—not listening, polishing her nails instead of looking at Effrain, turning to others, and being uninterested in her partner's ideas. This role-play was brief and enjoyed by all in the spirit intended—how not to be a partner!

Partners collected their materials, found places to sit, and began step 1, talking about the weather.

TRACY Would you like me to tell you a story about what happened to me one time in a tornado?

JON Yes!

TRACY But first, let's talk. I like it when the sun is shining. What do you like?

JON I like it when it is raining and you get all wet.

TRACY Want me to tell you about the tornado now? One day the tornado sucked up the rainbow and a piece of it fell off and there was enough of it for me to make a headband.

JON Well, do you know that one day when Little Red Riding Hood was playing in the snow, me and my uncle visited her on a sled?

KARLA Your stories about the weather are very interesting. Do you think you will be able to begin writing soon?

The recess bell gave children a short break outside, and then before they resumed their poems, Karla brought them together on the community mat.

KARLA I heard lots of people talking to their partner about ideas. I heard people saying "You go first" and "Which one do you want?" I saw people helping their partner to spell words. I heard people asking their partner to spell words. I saw people who were sharing markers. So I saw a lot of kind, fair partners!

Now I am going to put you into foursomes so you can share your sentences.

JEREMY You tell your sentence to them, right?

KARLA Right. And remember how you all have to agree where to put each person's sentence to make the poem? *(Adding step 5 to the board)*

Do you remember that we also made pictures to go with our poems? *(Adding step 6)*

Who has ideas about how to be kind group members?

CHERYL   You can ask them if they would like you to help them draw the pictures.

TRACY   You could let them go first.

JON   If you want to share the glue, the people could mark where they want their sentence to go on the paper and then glue it on.

Helping children relate their ideas to fairness, Karla then had partnerships pair up and take a large poster on which to put their sentence strips.

One group carefully carried their large poster among the four of them toward a space on the floor. Deirdre returned to the supply shelf and got one glue bottle for the group.

VANESSA   There is room for everybody if we move over.

KEVIN   First we have to read our sentences. Can I do mine first?

VANESSA   Okay.

DEIRDRE   *(Nods)*

JEREMY   I want to go next. But I can't read.

VANESSA   I'll read it for you.

After all the sentences were read, each child negotiated where to place his or her sentence on the poster. They left the space in the middle for their drawings.

A second group had spent time debating who would carry the poster. Finally they decided that two of them would carry the poster and two would carry the four glue bottles.

CRYSTAL   We have got to share these markers.

ANTHONY   Hey, let's glue like this.

Chris started to bring a chair to sit on.

SABRINA   Don't bring chairs. We can do it on the floor.

ANTHONY   Let's glue them like this. *(He began to glue his sentence strip on an outside edge of the paper)* Put them along the side so you have room in the middle.

The others followed suit and then divided the middle space into four boxes, in which they each drew their own illustration.

KARLA   *(Stopping by)* How did you decide where to put the sentences?

CRYSTAL   We let Anthony go first, and then Chris, and then Sabrina, and I was last.

Around the room, groups had approached the task in different ways. Some had put their sentence strips around the edge of the posters; others had put them in traditional verse sequence. Three groups had drawn lines defining each person's drawing space; four had not defined boundaries between their drawings. In the groups where children shared the common space, many helped each other with their illustrations or even worked toward one large picture.

JON   I'm scared of real tornadoes.

TRACY   *(Adding a second tornado to the border of the poster)* I'm not.

DANIEL   I'm scared a little bit when I see tornadoes.

TRACY   Okay, here is a mother tornado and a father tornado. I am going to put lots of tornadoes.

JON   No! Only two!

DANIEL   Three, okay? One for the baby.

TRACY   Do you want to help me do a baby tornado, Ashley?

The foursome put their heads together and all helped with the coloring.

KARLA   One more minute, guys, one more minute.

Children put away their materials and brought their finished products to the mat for sharing. Karla reminded children that they could choose to read their own poems or have her read them. After the poems were shared, Karla asked children to reflect on ways they had been kind and fair with each other.

CRYSTAL I shared the markers with the whole group.

ANTHONY I helped Chris do something and then he liked it. And they said I could go first and that made me feel good.

ROBERT   Jesse needed some help, and I helped him.

KARLA   Did any group have a problem and work on solving it? Tell us what the problem was and tell us how you solved it.

DANIEL   Well, the girls were complaining who was going to go first.

KARLA   How did you work it out?

TRACY   I said, "Why don't we put them in the center so it will look like we all went first?"

ASHLEY   And we all got a glue bottle so we all could go first.

SOME POINTS TO CONSIDER

✔ Karla had two goals—one academic and one social—for this lesson, and she was able to meet both of them using a Group Poetry format. Academically, her children's writing experience had been largely limited to journals and class books, and she wanted to give them more experience writing in a different form: poetry. Socially, the children's group work had been largely limited to partnerships, and she wanted to give them more experience negotiating the challenges inherent in working with larger groups.

✔ During all three parts of the lesson—introduction, group work, and reflection—Karla helped children focus on both their academic and social learning:

Introduction. Karla established an audience and a purpose for the writing activity: the children would be making weather poem posters for their parents to view. She prepared children for the academic content of their task by having them remember their recent weather learning and experiences, and by reminding them of the poem form of writing they had used once before, after seeing *The Twelve Sleeping Princesses.* She prepared them for the social goal of working kindly by role-playing partner interactions, both kind and unkind, with Johanna and Effrain.

Student Groups. Because children were familiar with the task directions, they were able to focus on making decisions about how to interact and what to write.

In Karla Moore's first grade, a focus on social goals as well as academic goals contributes to a harmonious classroom.

Developmentally, of course, the groups differed. Some made more collaborative choices than others, such as picking up one glue bottle rather than four; some interacted more collaboratively, such as Tracy's group when they negotiated tornado quantities and placement; and some made more interesting or elaborate poem posters. But not one group was sidetracked by the confusion and frustration of not knowing what to do.

Teacher Observation. As Karla moved around the room, she asked questions to get students on track—she refocused Tracy and Jon, for example, from their tall tales to their writing task. Karla also made note of specific student behaviors to report back to the class—for example, the asking of solicitous questions and widespread helpfulness with each others' spelling problems. And she asked questions to get at students' decision-making processes—for example, when she asked Crystal's group how they decided on the arrangement of their sentences.

Class Reflection. Because this activity was a relatively long process for her first-graders, Karla brought the class together midpoint to reflect back to them some of the kind behaviors she was observing and to help them transition from partner to group work.

To conclude the lesson, Karla had groups come together and share their poem posters and their learning. Since many children were very "early" readers and writers, Karla gave each group the choice of whether to read their own poem or to have her read it. Just as she had chosen the Group Poetry format because it allowed children to be successful at their own particular ability level, Karla also made sure they could be successful during the sharing. As the children reflected on the ways they had been kind and fair, Karla encouraged them to discuss problems they encountered as well as successes they enjoyed.

When Should an Activity Be Collaborative?

Several considerations are implicit in the design of collaborative formats, and should be accounted for in designing any collaborative lesson or experience—even when the "design" is a spur-of-the-moment decision to have students turn to a partner and tell their idea.

Many of the activities you currently use with children individually may, with minimal adaptation, be appropriate for collaboration. At the same time, however, there is little point in making an individual activity a collaborative one unless some clear benefits can be achieved through collaboration. What criteria might help you decide whether to structure a learning activity as a collaborative one? While our list of guiding questions is not exhaustive, the following points may be helpful to keep in mind as you design your own collaborative experiences for children:

1. *Will the learning be a stretch for students?*
   If the learning in an activity is challenging, the security and support of a small group can encourage children to take the risks that often accompany new learning. Shared responsibility can bolster students' willingness to experiment with ideas and to articulate them. It is often easier for students to share their thinking in a small group than to do so as individuals in the larger class, whether the process is writing or discussion.

2. *Is the activity a big one—in size or scope?*
   A task that is a big or even overwhelming undertaking for one person can be a natural for collaboration. Making a mural, for example, could become tedious for one child but is easily managed by several. Investigating all the planets of the solar system might be beyond any individual child, but small groups of children could each investigate a single planet and make a report to the class.

3. *Will a variety of ideas be important?*
   Arriving at a variety of ideas is often the first step in a discussion or activity. An individual child may not generate many ideas alone, but brainstorming allows children to hear the ideas of others, which can spark their own thinking.

4. *Will a variety of solutions or perspectives enrich the learning or product?*
   Through the give and take of discussion, explanation, and hearing different perspectives, children's thinking and learning are enhanced. If an activity is open-ended enough to allow for different processes, strategies, and solutions, the act of comparing and evaluating those strategies and solutions deepens children's understanding and enhances their thinking abilities. Similarly, if an activity allows for different perspectives, children not only learn from articulating and justifying their own positions, but they also become aware that multiple perspectives and opinions are possible.

5. *Do children's differing skills and abilities require different ways for them to be successful?*
   When children have quite different talents and skills, a multifaceted, flexible, and open-ended collaborative activity can enable each child to make valuable contributions. "Multiple-abilities tasks," as they are called by cooperative learning researcher and curriculum designer Elizabeth Cohen,* allow for different kinds of participation and encourage children to lead in areas where they are more capable and learn from peers in areas where they are less capable.

---

* *Finding Out/Descubrimiento* is an elementary school science curriculum that Cohen designed for use with multi-lingual, multi-ability groups. She is also the author of *Designing Groupwork: Strategies for the Heterogeneous Classroom* (Teachers College Press, 1986).

Forming Groups

THE DECISIONS we make about grouping play an important part in the relative success of our students' experience of collaborative activities. For a given activity, we might find that children are working in groups that are too small or too new or too homogeneous, while for another activity, small, new, and homogeneous are just what's called for.

Our decisions about grouping depend on our (sometimes competing) goals for an activity—whether it is most important to provide for children's autonomy, maximize learner success, provide optimal challenge, establish an inclusive community, or learn about children's interpersonal styles and skills. Consider how each of these goals might be promoted, or not, with the three methods of forming groups: teacher selection, random matching, and student selection.

In the beginning of the year, some special considerations mitigate against one method of forming groups—student selection. Letting children choose their own partners at this time may inadvertently promote high regard for similarity—since children naturally gravitate toward others who are *like* them—instead of promoting high regard for a friendly and respectful climate that is grounded in an appreciation for differences.

Especially in situations where children have not been used to class norms of kindness and respect and have not been used to working with everyone in the room, it's common for them to feel that partnering with anyone other than their personal choice is onerous—even undoable. When children have classroom "enemies," when gender-bashing is prevalent, or when cliques set the tone for social relationships, it is especially important to take the time, from the very first days of school, for students to work in partnerships and small groups with *all* of their peers in a variety of activities.

 Who Else Does Not Have a Partner?

In the activity below, Deborah Claypool had spent lots of time helping her grade one-two students get to know one another, a friendly climate was in place, and Deborah was interested in seeing how well children would be able to make responsible partnering decisions for themselves.

The students had each written a story. Deborah discussed with the class how partners could help each other revise their stories. She modeled peer-conferencing for them. Then she asked them to think about what would make a good conferencing partnership. Deborah invited the children to suggest how best to form those partnerships. After offering several ideas, children decided that on this day they would choose their own partners.

Many children made a beeline to each other. Others looked around and waited anxiously for someone to choose them. Deborah helped Sherman find someone to work with. Gradually the throng cleared, and almost all of the children had moved off to a work space with their chosen partner. Four lone figures were still standing on the carpet, however.

"I wanted to work with Kevin," Jeffrey told Deborah in a sad voice.

"Kevin is already set up, Jeffrey. Who else does not have a partner?"

Two of the three other boys took a step toward Deborah and Jeffrey. Daniel remained where he was, with his head down and his thumb in his mouth.

Gathering the four around her, Deborah tried to help them figure out two partnerships. But each of the four wanted to work with a different person than the one who wanted to work with him. Finally Deborah declared them a four-person partnership and they unhappily moved off to a table together.

Jeffrey and Alan eventually began to work. Roland spent most of his time looking around the room. Daniel kept his head down.

At the end of the day, Deborah and Joan reflected on what had happened.

JOAN   Can you talk a bit about the ways you group children?

DEBORAH   We do a whole lot of things, depending. Sometimes I decide, sometimes we draw colored pegs from a bucket, and today I thought they could group themselves. We have done a lot of talking about how we are all friends in here and how we need to be able to work with all our friends, not just our special friends. I was hoping they would be able to choose someone good for conferencing with on their writing, not necessarily a special friend.

JOAN   Many children seemed able to do that very successfully. Some seemed to need quite a bit of help to form a partnership.

DEBORAH   For the most part I was pleased with who they paired up with. The only problem was the four boys who were left till last. They really lack confidence and their skills are less developed than most of the others'.

JOAN   If I were a child lacking in confidence, I might find it really hard to ask someone to be my partner. It can take a lot of courage, and even young children can know when they are not as competent as other children in a particular area.

DEBORAH I did not think about *why* that group was left. I was just thinking, "That group cannot get it together. There is no leader in there." I didn't think about how having children chose partners can be a real risky thing for some of them to do.

SOME POINTS TO CONSIDER

✔ Because Deborah had spent time focusing children on the partner's responsibilities and what would lead to a successful conferencing partnership, she wanted to give children the autonomy to choose their own partners. The result was mixed. Some students made a beeline for their special friends; some refrained from simply choosing a special friend; and four boys were left stranded on the carpet.

When a collaborative activity focuses on specific academic skills, there is a special burden in allowing students to choose their own partners, since children who are less competent in those skills may be avoided by their peers and may also lack the confidence to invite anyone to partner with them.

✔ A less risky way to give children autonomy in forming groups is to limit student selection of groups to times when they are forming interest groups. That way there is a better chance that children will choose topics rather than personalities or competencies as the basis for forming groups.

Deborah Claypool's students discuss the responsibilities of being a partner and why it's important to be able to work with people who aren't just our "special friends."

Random and Teacher-Selected Groups

As Deborah mentioned, in addition to student selection she uses two other ways to form groups—random grouping and teacher selection. Random grouping is efficient and it can be fun. It also helps to emphasize the importance of every child learning to work with every other child in the class. Particularly in the beginning of the year, when we have little firsthand knowledge of our students and our students don't know each other very well, this is an extremely useful strategy.

As we get to know our children, we often find ways to optimize their learning by selecting their learning partners. For example, a highly creative child who has trouble keeping sufficiently focused to complete tasks may benefit from being paired with an efficient and task-oriented child, and vice versa. Two shy and tentative children may gain confidence by working together. A child who is fearful of children of the opposite gender may be helped to overcome this response by working with someone who is opposite in gender but shares many of his or her characteristics, and so on.

A cross between random and teacher-selected groups is sometimes appropriate. For example, in planning a cooperative activity and randomly grouping children in advance, we may want to change a few of the placements that come up, to better meet the needs of particular children.

This does not mean that we need to engage in continual matchmaking! Most children will be able to work just fine together in random groups, and as the year progresses even the children who have particular difficulties will be developing the skills and attitudes to work successfully within a wider variety of social situations.

Teachers Laurel Cress and Laura Ecken, who have years of experience putting students into collaborative groups, described some of their considerations in grouping students.

JOAN   Laurel—I know you don't need much prompting—why are you such an advocate of heterogeneous groups?

LAUREL When children work in heterogeneous groups they come face to face with different learning styles, different academic abilities, different levels of language and knowledge. They get involved in working with the opposite sex and different cultures. They come into contact with all the differences that are possible in other people—and that is learning in itself.

They learn how to give help and how to ask for help. They learn how to contribute their talents and skills, to use them in combination with the abilities and skills of others. They hear different ideas and viewpoints and their thinking is expanded in many more directions than if they only heard ideas similar to their own. I believe it is the richness of the learning from others that promotes their own.

JOAN   What are some times when the advantages of random, heterogeneous groups are outweighed by other considerations?

LAURA   For academic lessons and partner reading, I select the partnerships. I try to pair the children up so that they are academically linked—not the same, but where there is not a huge difference. I try to partner up children where I know that each person is going to have something to offer and that both will feel that they are putting something in, but that they are also getting something out.

When I first started using partners for academic lessons and reading, I tried to take a very capable, verbal student and put that student with a less capable, non-verbal student. It worked for a little while, but then what happened was that those very capable students would shut down the partnership—they just took over. It became obvious that it wasn't a fair partnership. In a partnership you have to feel that you are being challenged and getting something back.

SOME POINTS TO CONSIDER

✔ Heterogeneous groups work best when a learning activity requires several skills or talents in somewhat equal balance. Then differences, even large differences in one or two skills, can result in productive learning experiences for all children, as long as each can make meaningful contributions to the task.

✔ Laura's experience confirms that if a learning activity draws primarily on one skill or ability—reading, for example—then extreme differences in ability can lead the more advanced child to feel bored or impatient, and the less advanced child to feel unduly anxious and embarrassed.

Size of Groups

IN ADDITION TO making informed decisions about group formation and membership, it is essential to think about the size of the group. Groups of two, three, or four are the ideal size for elementary-aged children. Larger groups are less successful, unless the task easily divides into many subtasks.

 Partnerships Lay a Crucial Foundation

Many teachers find that the student-to-student relationships that are so important in a collaborative classroom can best be nurtured in partnerships. Especially in the beginning of the year, partnerships provide a safe way for children to build trusting relationships, learn and enhance cooperative skills, take risks in their learning, and develop confidence.

Though partnerships are used especially often with younger children, partner work is also the best choice for older, more experienced children when they don't know or trust each other well, when they need focused work on their collaborative skills, or when the learning task requires very complex integration of students' thinking.

In conversations excerpted below, teachers Fran Zimmerman, Laura Havis, Cindy Brooks, and Terry Rice, whose students range from first- to sixth-graders, described what they like about partnerships.

FRAN   With my first-graders there are very few times when I take them into groups larger than pairs. Partners are very important for young children. Having to negotiate with one person can be more than enough! Of course, along with partnerships we do whole-class projects where everyone contributes a part to the whole.*

---

* When a task requires a lot of negotiation and complex coordination, young learners in groups larger than two are apt to struggle. However, when the structure of tasks is simple, five- and six-year-olds are quite able to work successfully in groups larger than two. For example, if a task requires limited coordination, such as building with blocks or creating a collage, even young children can manage successfully to work in groups together. Young children can also succeed in groups larger than two when the coordination is built in, such as in playing a game or acting out a well-known story.

TERRY   My sixth-graders really benefit from partnerships. I always begin the year with whole-class activities focused on building unity and lots of partner activities. We do partner interviews, for example, about "Things I like and things I don't like." Students share out or make things on their partner's behalf. The idea is to get to understand each other better.

LAURA   At the beginning of the year I do partner chats and paired interviews. My original cooperative learning training was in groups of four, though I see now why pairs are so important. Pairs help students establish relationships and show them how to interact together.

CINDY   To me it doesn't matter whether children are in kindergarten or sixth grade, they need to build trust and learn to work with one other person before you expect them to be comfortable in larger groups. Along with whole-class, relationship-building activities, I believe that partnerships lay a crucial foundation if you want to develop a cooperative class.

SOME POINTS TO CONSIDER

✔ These teachers agree that partner work helps students build trusting relationships, no matter what the children's ages.

✔ Teachers also point out that the practice children get collaborating with a partner makes it easier for them to then negotiate the more complex demands of a larger group. Partnerships are a good way for children to prepare for group work.

 ## Groups of Three or Four Add Challenge

While partnerships foster caring relationships and help children learn to work with other people, larger groups are a powerful way to maximize children's learning. In a group of four, for example, children's thinking is stretched by being exposed to and having to accommodate a greater number of ideas and viewpoints. Groups provide greater scope for negotiation, planning, decision making, and problem solving. In general, groups increase the challenge in the learning taking place, and challenge is an essential ingredient in any effective community of learners.

More challenge, of course, means more potential for difficulties to arise. The bigger the group, the more relationships there are to manage, and the greater the skill required to work together effectively. This is particularly true when complex learning is involved. It is also generally true that the larger the group, the longer the time that will be needed. The success of groups larger than two needs to be thoughtfully planned for, especially when children have limited experience working in this way.

For example, when Cindy Brooks's fifth- and sixth-graders were about to embark on a video animation project, all of their previous collaborative learning had been done in partnerships; this was the first time they would be working in small groups. Cindy knew that the project would be challenging and would involve much learning for everyone. The notions of shared responsibility and shared contribution to the whole would be important and ongoing parts of that learning. So Cindy took some time to set a context in which group members could think about themselves and each other as people who can make a contribution.

First in partnerships within the group of four and then within the full group, children described what important gifts or contributions they would like to make to their family, their country, and the world. Their ideas were combined in a group shamrock, and then the class came together to discuss this first taste of working in groups of four.

Some children observed that working in a twosome was easier and better because there were fewer people; others thought that working in a larger group was better because there were more ideas. But most agreed that a larger group was more challenging; for students new to group work, just this simple awareness could boost their willingness to try hard and be forgiving.

SOME POINTS TO CONSIDER

✔ Because Cindy was forming groups that would work on this project together for several weeks, she began by providing group members with a way to get to know each other better.

✔ The information Cindy's students learned about each other established a positive sense of each group as a collection of people who wanted to contribute. This concept of "contributing" would be an important social learning focus during the making of the animations.

✔ Cindy's students were new to groups of four, so she started them off with a familiar partner interview activity before having them make any decisions as a group. When students are just beginning to work in groups of four, if there are appropriate subtasks that can be done by partnerships, it helps to leaven the new structure of group work with the familiar structure of partner work.

✔ Cindy gave students the relatively simple shamrock activity to start with because she wanted to be sure their first group experience would be successful. If her students were already experienced working in groups, she might have chosen a more complex getting-to-know-our-group activity.

✔ Cindy gave students a chance to reflect on the process of working together. As groups explore the animation task in the next few weeks, it will be important for Cindy to periodically take time to help them anticipate the challenges of working together and reflect on what they can do to make their group work successful.

Duration of Groups

A S WITH ALL decisions, determining the duration of groups depends on our purpose. During the period when we are getting to know our children, and they are getting to know each other and the importance of being able to work with all of their classroom peers, it is best to change partnerships or groups frequently—at least daily—and to use activities like partner interviews in which much of the coordination is contained in the nature of the task itself.

When we want children's collaboration to take them beyond getting comfortable with each other—even sometimes to the point of being *uncomfortable* with each other—we design activities that challenge them to understand and respect difference, to learn from and accommodate the ideas and perspectives of others, and to work through and resolve the inevitable "rough spots" as they arise. Such learning experiences necessitate keeping groups together for longer periods, sometimes as long as three or four weeks.

And, of course, informal or short-term partnerships can operate side-by-side with longer-term groups. The partners who help each other edit an essay one morning are independent of the groups working on a three-week project in the afternoons.

 These Past Three Weeks

What do students think about all the grouping decisions they experience? Brenda Henderson asked her fourth-graders, as they were winding up a three-week group project.

BRENDA   You have been working in the same groups of four these past three weeks. Why do you think that I might now want to switch groups around?

SHONTÉ   So you can get to know other people better and get a chance to work with others.

PAUL   When you are in a new group, then you do new things.

SHERRY   If you are having trouble in one group, you might not in another one.

RAISA   You can see how a group is different than the group you were in.

CARSON   And maybe you are different in a different group, too.

SHEILA   You can get to meet other people instead of staying with the people you have always been with. So you learn more.

JESSE   You can learn how to work with them and learn to be better friends with them.

IRENE   This is what I think. I think sometimes if we are with a group that is laughing, then you switch us the next time so we do not get our feelings hurt.

HANK   If we are having problems with the people around us you can try us out with other people and see if that works out.

TINA   You can have people that listen and people that do not listen. You can put them together so the people who can listen can help the others.

SOME POINTS TO CONSIDER

✔ As Brenda's students demonstrated, children can be quite sophisticated in what they understand about grouping decisions. When we clarify with children the purposes for which groups form, and how long they will be together, children are less likely to want "out" from a group or to want another group member "out." Children benefit from understanding that they are together for "the duration," but that it is only *one* duration.

✔ Before Brenda disbands the current groups, she will provide an opportunity for them to reflect on and celebrate what they have learned—academically and socially—during the time they have spent together.

■

In this chapter we have looked at some of the major variables in designing group work—and the role of familiar formats in controlling one of those variables.

As we will see in the next chapter, most variables are introduced by the children themselves. Sometimes these result in "rough spots"—or, as some would say, more ways to learn about the dynamics of collaboration!

Rough Spots

WHEN WE ASK CHILDREN TO REFLECT ON their work, we ask them to consider both their successes and their challenges. Often it is the challenges that offer the most potential for learning. In collaborative groups these challenges may be experienced as "rough spots" that we as well as the children can analyze and learn from.

Problem Solving with Children

WHAT HAPPENS IF a collaborative group just doesn't work out? We know this is a possibility even when we have made thoughtful decisions about grouping and the activity is intrinsically interesting to children, appropriate for collaborative work, and neither too hard nor too easy for the individual group members.

Collaboration can be hard. Even a highly skilled adult group may experience conflict during their work together. But what adults generally have that children are still developing are the interpersonal skills and necessary attitudes to work out their conflicts. Children need the opportunity to learn these skills and attitudes, with as much of our support as is necessary, and in a way that helps them take as much ownership and responsibility for their learning as they are able.

As children are given and take on increasing control over themselves and their actions, they not only grow in self-confidence, but they also become more committed to their learning. As they develop this stronger sense of autonomy and inner direction, they are more able to work with others and build healthy relationships in an interdependent, rather than dependent, way.

Talking over "rough spots" is a way for everyone to learn.

As with most worthwhile learning, this takes time, some mistakes, practice, feedback, reflection, and an ongoing focus on prosocial values and skills. The teachers we visit in this book understand these things and, perhaps most important, are prepared to work consistently over time toward helping children learn to become more responsible. In the scene below, Laura Ecken works with three of her seven- and eight-year-olds, helping them turn a rough spot into a success.

 ## What Could You Do Next Time?

The children had enjoyed listening to the book *Miss Maggie* and discussing the unlikely friendship between the old woman and her young neighbor, Nat. To further the children's understanding of the story characters, Laura asked them to work in partnerships to write a dialogue between Miss Maggie and Nat.

LAURA   Before you go off to work on your dialogues, what are some of the things we need to remember about working in a partnership?

ROBIN   Find a quiet place to work.

STELLA   Do not sit back and let the other person do all the writing and thinking.

HARRY   Be fair.

Laura used the children's comments to help clarify what this meant for working in their partnerships—for example, how they would make decisions and share the work.

After forty-five minutes or so, partnerships were at varied points in their task, but only the threesome of Frank, Philip, and Brandon had accomplished nothing. A few students were deciding who would do what, some were writing out their dialogue, and some were at the point of practicing their role-play. Laura called the class together.

LAURA   I know that you are not finished, but I would like us to talk a little bit about your partnerships before we go to lunch. What has been going well?

SHELLY   We were fair.

LAURA   Can you tell us a way that you and your partner were fair?

SHELLY   We worked it out.

LAURA   What did you work out?

SHELLY   He wrote some and I wrote some.

After children contributed more examples of successes in their partnerships, Laura asked them to describe some of the difficulties they had encountered.

LAURA   Let's talk about some of the problems you are having, some of the rough spots.

SUKIE   We had trouble at first deciding which words we were going to put down because we wanted to write different things.

LAURA   How did you work it out?

SUKIE   We listened to each other and then chose what we both liked.

FRANK   Brandon and Philip were talking about Nintendo and stuff.

LAURA   How did that make you feel?

FRANK   Sad, because they were not paying attention to what I wanted to say. Mad, too.

LAURA   Philip, how did you feel about the way the partnership worked?

PHILIP   *(No response)*

LAURA   Brandon, how did you feel about the way the partnership worked?

BRANDON   *(No response)*

LAURA   Frank, what did you do to get the partnership back together again?

FRANK   *(No response)*

LAURA   Did you all get anything accomplished?

BOYS   *(All three shook their heads; no one said anything)*

LAURA   What suggestions do any of the rest of you have so they can go ahead tomorrow and get their dialogue written?

HANNAH   Say, "I want you to listen to me."

DEREK   You can say, "You did not listen to me so I am not going to listen to you."

LAURA   Is that going to help get the assignment done?

LARRY   You could tell the teacher.

LAURA   I guess you can . . . if you get to the point where you cannot do it and you have given it your best effort, then maybe the teacher can come over and give a suggestion.

          Brandon, what do you think you can do tomorrow to make the partnership work?

BRANDON   *(Protesting)* I did not do anything!

LAURA   But that is not fair in a partnership—not to do anything.

BRANDON	It was Philip's fault. He kept taking my pencils.
LAURA	Philip, can you think of something you can do tomorrow to try and make the partnership work better—to contribute to the partnership?
PHILIP	I am going to try to listen.
LAURA	Frank, can you think of something you can do tomorrow to try and make the partnership work better?
FRANK	I'll try to work it out together.
LAURA	Brandon, what about you?
BRANDON	*(No response)*
LAURA	Does anyone have a suggestion for Brandon?
RAY	Yes, they can take turns and just have one clipboard and share a pencil.
LAURA	Yes, maybe there were too many materials over there.
TOM	Why don't you try talking about it before you get involved with the pencils?
RAMON	I had a rough spot, thinking of what to do to get started.
LAURA	So, how did you solve your problem?
RAMON	Sukie gave us a suggestion of something Miss Maggie might say, so we could get started.
LAURA	So, giving a suggestion helped. Okay, thank you all for your comments. Try to use some of these ideas to make your partnerships work better tomorrow.

Problem Solving with Frank, Brandon, and Philip

The next afternoon as partnerships resumed work on their dialogues, Laura met with Frank, Brandon, and Philip.

LAURA	Yesterday when we were sharing, we had a long talk about what went well in our partnerships and what were some of the rough spots, and one of the rough spots that you all had was you didn't get started. What do you think was the problem?
BRANDON	That, that they was talking about Nintendo.
PHILIP	Not! 'Cause we been talking about the paper.
BRANDON	*(Pointing at Frank)* Wasn't he talking about some other things, too?
FRANK	*(Shaking his head)*
BRANDON	Uh huh!
LAURA	Okay, well Brandon what do you think . . .

BRANDON They blaming it all on me!

LAURA No, no. This paper has everybody's name on it and there's nothing written. So it's like everybody's responsible, okay? It's like Frank didn't get anything done yesterday, Brandon didn't get anything done, and Philip didn't get anything done.

BRANDON See, watch this. *(To Frank)* Did you do anything? Huh?

FRANK *(Shaking his head)*

BRANDON *(Pointing at Philip)* Did he do anything?

FRANK *(Shaking his head again)*

BRANDON See, they blaming it all on me!

FRANK He was talking about Nintendo.

BRANDON I don't even have no 'intendo!

LAURA Okay, well let's look at it this way. Frank, did you do anything to help the assignment?

FRANK I tried to.

LAURA You tried to. What did you do to help with the assignment?

FRANK I kept telling him to listen and stuff.

LAURA Brandon, did you do anything to help the assignment? To get the assignment started? What did you do?

BRANDON I was, I was telling 'em to just to stop playing around and stop taking stuff from me and stuff.

PHILIP He was the one playing around.

BRANDON It wasn't your turn!

LAURA Yes, let him talk, I did ask him. So you asked people to stop playing around?

BRANDON Yeah.

LAURA Okay. Philip, what did you do to try to help get the assignment going?

PHILIP Tried to tell him to stop so we could write, get something down on the piece of paper.

LAURA So it sounds like everybody kept telling everybody else what to do but nobody ever got started doing anything?

BOYS *(Nods and silence)*

LAURA Now one thing that I sort of noticed that I thought was a problem was where you chose to work—there were lots of distractions around the sink area. So today you can choose to work on the rug or you can choose to work at a table, where there aren't many distractions.

BRANDON *(Resentfully)* Well, why don't they . . . why do the other people get to sit any-place?

LAURA Well, Brandon, it seems like every single person got something done except this group, so I felt like I needed to make a suggestion to this group to help you get started. As the teacher, that's what my suggestion is—that you do not sit where you will be distracted, that you sit at a table or on the rug where you can concentrate. Okay?

BRANDON *(With dawning acceptance)* Okay.

LAURA Now, what else can you do to get the assignment done?

Listening to the boys' ideas, Laura helped them to clarify what they needed to do, what they would like to write about, and how they might include each person, since they were working as a threesome.

LAURA If you feel like you are getting in a bad way and you are trying to work it out but you are still having some rough spots, I'll be around—I'm available to help you.

As the boys began their work, having finally decided to sit on the rug, Laura watched from a distance. Philip fiddled with a small piece of wire that was lying on the rug. Frank tried to draw him into the group.

FRANK Do you agree with that one, Philip?

PHILIP *(Nods)*

FRANK Okay, who would you like to be?

PHILIP *(Looking unsure)*

FRANK You sound more like the kid.

PHILIP *(Brightening)*

BRANDON I want to be the kid!

FRANK You were the kid yesterday. Let him be the kid.

With a shrug Brandon removed the wire from the carpet and placed it on a nearby shelf, as if to signal, "If you are going to be the kid then you need to concentrate and do a good job."

Later, the class moved into a sharing circle, and volunteers performed their role-plays. As Steven and Jon stood up to do their role-play, they collapsed into giggles.

The children waited patiently.

LAURA   Boys, maybe you need to practice. You need to be serious because if you have worked really hard in your partnership, it does not feel really good if you go up to share and then you could not do it. Do you want to comment on that?

BOTH
BOYS   No.

LAURA   Okay, we will give you some more time to practice, and you can share out a little later.

Mary, Shelly, and Sukie performed their role-play next. When they were finished, Laura asked them to comment on their work together.

LAURA   Now, Mary was absent yesterday so she was new to the partnership today. How did you make her feel part of the partnership?

SHELLY We talked about it and let her decide what part she wanted to be.

LAURA   So you added another part so that everyone had a turn to speak?

SHELLY Yes.

LAURA   Brandon, Philip, and Frank, what would you all like to share?

The boys role-played what they had practiced, each taking a fairly equal part.

LAURA   Can you tell us how you worked three people into a two-person dialogue?

FRANK   I was thinking when we were talking before that we could have a grand-father.

LAURA   So you managed to work three people into the dialogue today—and every-body shared some thoughts about that?

BOYS   *(Pleased with themselves, they nod)*

LAURA   You did not get started yesterday and today you got it written, practiced, and performed.

FRANK   We thought about yesterday when we did not succeed, so we thought about it again. Today we worked real hard.

LAURA   Brandon and Philip, do you agree?

BOTH
BOYS   *(They nod and their classmates give them a spontaneous round of applause)*

LAURA   Any more rough spots?

JON   I wanted to write.

STEVEN	Well, he did not tell me he wanted to write until after I had finished!
LAURA	What could you do next time?
JON	Talk to my partner about it first and work it out together.
PETER	I did not like it when Larry was kicking the vent.
LAURA	Larry, what could you have done differently?
LARRY	*(Avoiding Laura's eyes)* Do not do it.
LAURA	I think it is very important to give people credit for telling about what did not go so well, because then we can talk about suggestions—that is kind of how we learn.

SOME POINTS TO CONSIDER

✔ Laura works on problem solving with children in two related ways. First, she works proactively to prevent or minimize the likelihood of problems occurring (or recurring). Laura had children plan for success in their partnerships by focusing on the process of working together. After their collaborative work she also invited children to describe ways they had succeeded as partners.

Second, she has a positive approach to helping children take responsibility for solving the problems that do arise. Rough spots are treated as learning opportunities. Laura invited open discussion of specific problems and encouraged children to take responsibility for solving them, with questions such as, "What could you do differently next time?" and "Does anyone have a suggestion?"

✔ Laura recognized that Brandon, Philip, and Frank needed extra attention if they were to be successful. She used a problem-solving approach that helped them recognize their responsibility for their own and each other's success, and she helped them rehearse specific actions they could take as group members. She never implied that there was any reason for them not to be successful.

A Problem-Solving Process for Children to Use

The problem-solving process Laura uses in her classroom is widely applicable and easy for even young children to learn and use—whether they are encountering a problem in their small group, reflecting as a whole class, or stuck with a personal problem to solve. Many teachers talk the steps through explicitly with children and post a chart of the steps for easy referral by everyone.

In addition to making problem-solving steps explicit, it is important to help children understand that not all problems are solved in one try.

1. *Define the problem.*
   This is the heart of problem solving—defining a problem instead of a culprit. In Brandon, Frank, and Philip's group, the problem was not that Brandon did or did not talk about Nintendo, but that the whole group never got started. It was a problem for everyone. Laura helped the boys define the problem, since they were unable to do so, but her long-range goal is for children to learn how to do it themselves.

2. *Generate possible solutions.*
   Laura helped the boys brainstorm ways that each of them needed to work to get the assignment done.

3. *Evaluate and decide on solutions.*
   Laura helped the boys clarify and decide how their ideas would help them, checked that they had all of the information they needed to begin, and left them to decide whether they would work on the rug or at a table. She also made it clear that she was available to support them should they need her assistance.

4. *Implement a plan of action.*
   As Philip, Frank, and Brandon put their ideas into practice, Laura observed them from a distance, so that she could monitor their success and intervene if necessary.

5. *Assess how well it worked.*
   Following their role-play presentation, Laura gave the boys feedback and the opportunity to make their own assessment of their work together.

When and How to Intervene

A big part of problem solving with children is knowing when and how to intervene. In conversations with Joan, teachers Laura Ecken, Laura Havis, and Brenda Henderson talked about their experiences learning how to help children find their way past rough spots.

JOAN   Do you have some general guidelines about when to intervene?

LAURA E. I watch for a little while and if I see a group is at a stalemate or off track, then I feel I need to go over to the kids and see what is going on. You cannot assume that you know why a group is not working.

When I intervene I want to help children take ownership of a problem and see that it is something they can work out. I'm there, but I try to let them come up with steps they can take to solve it.

JOAN   Do you mean, for example, like when you talked with Brandon, Philip, and Frank?

When a collaborative group is having a problem, Brenda Henderson finds that asking questions is the first step in helping children work out a solution.

LAURA E.   Yes. I wanted *them* to take responsibility for solving their problem. They wanted to blame everything on Brandon. No one wanted to take any responsibility. I also wanted to be sure they had some skills so that if it happened again they would think about what to do.

LAURA H.   I check things out in a group when I hear loud voices raised in argument. I also intervene if kids seem to have mentally left their group. I watch their body language and if I see kids moving away from each other, I check it out. Also, I have some very quiet, reserved children and I try to keep track of how they're getting along.

BRENDA   When it comes to intervening, I wait a lot more than I used to. Before I always wanted jump in and solve all their problems—I wanted to move children along. But then I began to realize that this was not in their best interests, and it was not collaborative learning—because to me part of collaborative learning means letting children work out the normal differences and obstacles they encounter.

My deciding factor is if anger is present, because I feel like anger fuzzies our ability to see what we need to see. If children are angry, then I usually join in the group, but if they've just got a rough spot and they're not angry and they seem to be working at it, I stay out of it.

When groups have rough spots, I might look, too, to see if I've missed something in designing or introducing the task—whether it is unclear or whether the task is inappropriate.

JOAN   Once you've decided to intervene, how do you approach a group?

LAURA H.   I'll usually ask an open-ended question like "What's happening here?" or I'll focus them on something I have noticed.

Recently when we were working together in groups, three children in one group had their back to the fourth, one of the quiet ones. I watched how they had almost closed her out because she wasn't saying anything. It was like they had decided that it was easier to work that way, and she wasn't going to force herself into the group because that's not her style.

So I said to the group, "Take a look at what's happening. We have three people hard at work on the assignment. But I'm concerned because there are four people in this group. So what is Lashonda doing? Look at where you are facing." I helped them become aware of what their body language was doing to Lashonda, and they decided how they would change that to include her.

BRENDA   When I approach a group, usually I just ask what do they feel that the problem is, and I ask each child to tell how they see it—uninterrupted. Then I ask them what they think they can do to solve it, and they come up with suggestions. I tell them they have to be able to live with whatever they decide—it doesn't have to be the solution they want most, but they have to be able to live with it.

JOAN   What do you do when the problem seems to be more related to one child than to the group?

LAURA H.   Last week Charlene was having a tough time in her group and she came to me complaining that no one was doing what she wanted. I said, "What makes you think that they *should*?" She looked at me as if I was crazy. Finally I said, "Charlene, you have to be able to tell your *partners*—I'm just a person standing on the outside. If you're having difficulties, you need to talk it through with them." I could see she was thinking, "You're the teacher, you should be over there."

Today when she worked with her group, I heard her begin with the comment, "Before we start we have to decide who's going to do what." So she had made some decisions for herself, like, "I'm not going to get myself in the same situation I was in last time. Let's work out what we're going to do here."

That is something that I really work on doing—even when it's one child having a problem—I try to have children solve as much as they can themselves, within the group.

BRENDA   When it's the case of one student who isn't contributing to the group, I will ask that child whether he has been given something that he isn't comfortable with, or I'll try to find out if it's something he doesn't know how to do, or I'll ask him to suggest a way he would like to contribute to the activity.

I ran into this just the other day when a boy said he was not going to do the activity, that he did not care, and that he was just going to sit out in the hall! When I went outside the door to talk to him, I just asked him, "Do you really not care?" He started crying, "I care, but I just said that because I didn't want to look stupid." In his case I found out the task was too hard for him.

So this is how I have learned not to be heavy-handed. Before I would have just told him what he was supposed to do, I wouldn't have asked him. I would have said, "You're not trying hard enough—you need to care!" I would have told him all the things he needed to do. Well, of course, he does care. And that has been my learning!

JOAN   Are there times when a problem becomes something you want to talk over with the whole class?

LAURA E.   When groups end up coming to me, or I notice problems lots of people are having, we have a class meeting and talk about situations that happen in groups—like what could you do if somebody does not want to participate, or if people are just talking about TV last night, or if somebody will not let you take part because they want to do the whole thing themselves.

One of the things we came up with is telling people how you feel. Part of problem solving is being able to say how you feel. So we said if someone's taking over the work, for example, you could say, "I feel sad because I feel like you are not letting me do anything." Then we talked about if you're the person someone said it to, what you might think and what you might do.

The kids suggest situations that are very real, and we have even brainstormed a chart of ideas to handle these situations without involving the teacher.

LAURA H.   Just today we had a class discussion because I was talking with a group that was blaming one student for their problems. They were making excuses like "Oh, he doesn't know what to do" or "He's always fooling around." And I had been noticing that this has become a common issue, and therefore a class concern.

So our question for the discussion was "What do we do when people don't want to do the assignment, and they do all kinds of things to try to pull us off task?"

I raised questions about whose responsibility it is—mine, the group's, the child's? We came to agreement that we all share responsibility for helping the child to participate, but that students would try to work it out within their group before asking me to help. We talked about what could we do to make the child feel like they're part of the group.

JOAN   What if a group says something like "We do not want to work with Anthony"?

LAURA E.   Well, I would hope we had done enough work before that so that it would not come up. In the beginning of the year Mr. B. [the support teacher] and I role-played things like "I do not want to work with you." And I asked Mr. B., "How did you feel when I said that to you?"

Then I asked the kids, "How did you feel when you heard me talk to Mr. B. that way? Do unkind words hurt just the people they are being said to?" We talked as a class about how everybody is hurt by unkind words. We related back to our class norms of kindness and consideration, fairness, and responsibility.

SOME POINTS TO CONSIDER

✔ Brenda, Laura Ecken, and Laura Havis described giving children the chance to solve social and academic problems in collaboration with their peers as a central goal of collaborative learning. They also pointed out that adult guidance is often necessary. Working in this way—giving students every opportunity to work out their own solutions, yet having the sensitivity and know-how to intervene when they need guidance—is a skill that develops gradually, with lots of experience.

✔ As all three teachers pointed out, we can't assume to know why a group isn't working or why one child is having a hard time. These teachers ask the children. This is the first step in finding a solution.

Adjusting the Lesson

A S WE ALL KNOW, there are times when the lesson or activity is itself the cause of problems. Children may be perfectly willing and able to cooperate on a task, but the task confounds their efforts. Often, small adjustments can turn a failed activity into a successful one.

 **No Response?**

In comparing the two scenes below, we will see that Cindy Brooks was able to analyze an activity that failed in the morning with one group of fifth-grade children and then refine it for a second group in the afternoon.

Three days into the school year, Cindy's math class assembled for the first time. This was a different group from the one assigned to Cindy for home room.

CINDY   Good morning everyone, and welcome to room 23 for math. I have lots of information to pass on to you, but I want to start out first with a unity builder so that you can feel comfortable with each other.

We're going to do a "four-corners" activity. I would like you to think about the math operations—addition, subtraction, multiplication, and division—and which one you're best at doing. *(Cindy identified each of the four corners of the room with one of the operations)* When you are in the corner that represents the one you are best at, discuss with the other people why you think that particular one is the one you can do the best. Is it easy? Do you enjoy doing it the most? Is it because you understand it?

SAM   I like doing multiplication, but not the bigger ones.

CINDY   Okay, that is something you can discuss in your group.

Fifteen children moved to the multiplication corner and stood uncertainly together, reluctant to start talking. Cindy moved to that corner to get a discussion going.

Meanwhile, in the three other corners, only the four girls who had decided on subtraction were actually engaged in conversation. In the division corner, the one girl moved away and stood with her back to the three boys, who simply watched what was happening elsewhere in the room. Some of the students in the addition corner discovered the air conditioning vent and, since it was a very warm day, split off from the rest of their group and cooled themselves!

Shortly, Cindy disengaged herself from the multiplication group and addressed the whole class.

CINDY   Can somebody share with me? How did that feel, discussing math? (*No response*) Was it easy? Was it hard?

DANIEL (*After a long silence*) It was kind of hard.

CINDY   Why?

DANIEL (*He shrugs; no one speaks*)

After lunch that day, Cindy met with her fifth-grade social studies class for the first time. Most of the children had not been in the morning math group.

CINDY   Welcome. My name is Mrs. Brooks and I will be having you for social studies this year.

Cindy gave children a brief overview of what they would be learning for the year, took attendance, told children some about herself, and answered their questions about her life outside of school.

CINDY   Okay. That is a bit about me, and I am looking forward to getting to know you over the school year.

Cindy explained that everyone would now do a four-corners activity to get to know each other some and find out where they lived in relation to other people in the class.

Cindy identified each corner with a direction—north, south, east, and west.

CINDY   When you get into the corner that is the direction you live in from the school, get into pairs and describe how to get to your house. Give very clear directions to your partner. Now, before we begin, what questions would you like to ask?

LUPE   What if you do not know the names of the streets?

CINDY   It is okay to say "over the field" or whatever, but I would like to hear some geography vocabulary. Okay, go ahead into your corners and then into your partnerships.

All the children participated, explaining in some form or another how to find their homes. Cindy called the class back together.

CINDY   How did you feel about the activity?

SHARIF   It was kind of fun to get to know where someone lives.

JESSICA   I never knew my partner lived that close to me.

ERIC   My partner found out that someone he likes lives near me.

ANGELA   It was pretty hard.

JESUS   It was interesting because I never had to give directions like that before.

 So, It Didn't Go As Planned

At the end of the day, Joan joined Cindy in the regular meeting Cindy and her colleague Lizbeth Nastari have each week. Cindy described for Lizbeth the two versions of the four-corners activity—and the adjustments she had made.

CINDY   This morning I met with my math group for the first time. I asked children to get into a corner that represented the math operation that they felt they were best at doing. And then when they got into corners they were supposed to talk and share information about why they thought that was their best strength.

There was one huge group—the multiplication group—and it was dead quiet. I thought, "I'll get the big group going and sharing and talking, and then I'll worry about the smaller groups." But the big group all turned to talk to me instead of to each other!

Jim Ketsdever

In Cindy Brooks's classroom, everyone benefits from her willingness to question herself as well as students, to analyze and learn from rough spots as well as successes.

And I could see the other groups, but I couldn't seem to get to them. In one, there were three boys and a girl, and the girl was standing with her back to them while the boys lounged around on the back cupboards. And in the addition group, half of them ended up under the air conditioning near my desk, so that was the topic of their discussion!

LIZBETH   So, it didn't go as planned.

CINDY   Right. They didn't have the terms—the vocabulary—to talk about "Why do you think this is your strength?" It was too hard for them. And I don't think they felt comfortable sharing their feelings about that with each other, either.

LIZBETH   I guess when they are meeting new people for the first time it's hard. On the other hand, now you know more about the level of comfort those kids need.

JOAN   Cindy, when you used the four-corners activity this afternoon with a different class, you seem to have planned differently. You changed some things.

CINDY   I had some time to think. I wasn't sure if the question this morning was wrong, or whether it was that the kids didn't know each other. Also, this morning I just got the kids straight into the activity. This afternoon I tried to get the kids feeling comfortable first by telling them a bit about myself and what they would be learning over the year. The other difference was that this afternoon they had to explain how to get to their house—it wasn't asking something like how do you feel about living north of the school.

LIZBETH It was something more concrete.

CINDY   Very.

JOAN   And it connected to their own personal knowledge. I noticed you did something else differently, too.

CINDY   Did I?

JOAN   You asked them to find and talk to a partner once they'd gotten into their corners.

CINDY   Yes, I thought of how big that multiplication group was, and how scary it might have been for kids. So I decided to combine a partner chat in this type of activity.

It felt so different from this morning where they were sort of shuffling and looking uncomfortable. I thought it went a lot better. And they really enjoyed finding out where people lived.

SOME POINTS TO CONSIDER

✔ Cindy recognized that there could have been many reasons why her first four-corners activity felt like a flop—and they were unrelated to misbehaving children. She examined not only elements of the activity, but also the context in which children were asked to do it.

✔ Cindy sees teaching as continuous learning. She is prepared to persist when things don't work as planned. In this instance, she reflected on what happened and why, made changes, and tried again.

■

In this chapter we have seen how students and teachers sometimes struggle, but are able to use such experiences for their own learning. As Cindy said to Lizbeth and Joan, "I'm constantly asking myself, 'Am I doing the right thing? Is there a better way?'"

And as we will see in the next chapter, being reflective hardly precludes achieving a comfortable level of confidence in the decisions we make in classrooms.

Getting Comfortable

As LEARNERS WE ARE ALWAYS STRIVING FOR coherence. That's what learners do. And when we find coherence, we experience a satisfying sense of well-being—the realization, "This makes sense to me, I am comfortable with it." In this book, we have visited a number of teachers, all of them learners, who are creating coherence between their academic goals for children and the goals they have for children to be kind, thoughtful, intrinsically motivated human beings. When the children in our care experience this kind of coherence, it goes a long way in helping them grow up to be the adults we would all want for neighbors or doctors or presidents.

Teacher Journeys

FOR SOME OF US, the professional journey we make is a gradual evolution of our thinking and practices; for others, there are points along the way at which we make a pronounced shift in how we organize instruction, relate to our students, or conceptualize our role. The teachers we have visited in this book represent both kinds of journeys as well as a combination of the two. It's to be expected that each of us will have a distinctive journey since each of us has his or her own personal starting point, style, and emphasis—even within a shared set of goals and values. The comments from the three teachers below provide a glimpse of how interesting these journeys can be.

 **Creeping Coherence!**

As Laurel Cress described below, sometimes coherence creeps into our practice before we are even aware of it. The tension between Laurel's personal need for control and her goal that children learn and take responsibility have caused a shift over the course of her career, as she is now quite aware.

LAUREL   When I was just starting out as a teacher, my first concerns were about classroom management. I didn't feel in control in the classroom and I was very tense when I taught, especially in the first two years. I had teacher nightmares, I got into power struggles with kids—and these were kindergartners! Assertive Discipline was popular then, and I used it.

Eventually I gave up Assertive Discipline for what you could call a problem-solving approach to discipline, and I also became interested in cooperative learning. When I thought about my classroom, I visualized one system in place for discipline and another system in place for cooperative learning. It didn't occur to me how they fit together—not until a couple years later when I was in a job interview. I was asked to write a short essay about how I prepare my class for cooperative learning. As I was organizing my answer, something hit me for the first time—the discipline system I was using was the *foundation* for the cooperative learning system I was using. It hadn't hit me before that all the work I did with kids creating class norms and emphasizing how we want to treat each other and how we solve problems—it was the foundation for everything that happened in my classroom, including cooperative learning. You know, now it seems so obvious, but that moment was a real breakthrough for me.

Also, as a beginning teacher, I had been very concerned with organization. I would pride myself on planning a three- or four-week unit at a time, without considering where the kids were. I could do October at a whole shot—and I would! People still stick me on wanting to outline everything for the kids. But I'm letting go of some of that. It's hard for me, but I'm doing it. And you know, it's like the discipline stuff. What's interesting is that when you do let go, the kids start initiating some of the responsibility. They are coming to me now with more of an assumption that I'm going to support what they want to do. It all builds together—they have more and more ideas because I am trusting them more to be responsible.

I listen more now, I talk more with the kids. I ask them what they think, and I ask them to share their ideas and thinking with each other. I am concerned with what the kids think and what is important to them—it is part of respecting them. And it is a big part of how a caring community happens.

When everyone counts, everyone can contribute. When everyone can contribute, everyone can learn.

SOME POINTS TO CONSIDER

✔ In the realm of classroom management, Laurel recognized that a discipline system built around teacher control did not fit with her goal of helping children learn to take responsibility.

✔ In the realm of academic instruction, it was harder for Laurel to recognize that she had a similar "responsibility" goal for children, and that it was being thwarted by her thorough but teacher-controlled lesson plans.

✔ Children helped Laurel create coherence between her social and academic goals for them. Once they learned that their teacher took them seriously on issues of social behavior, they simply expected that she would take them seriously on issues of academic behavior.

 Everyone Both Teacher and Learner

Like Laurel, Dawn Biscardi is an experienced teacher who still finds herself making changes so that her goals for children and her teaching practices are coherent.

DAWN   Making these shifts is not easy. There are those of us who have been in this business since dirt was formed, and becoming a facilitator is really very different than standing there telling children what you want them to do. But it is also very energizing when you suddenly begin to think about doing something in a different way. The minute I began to shift my thinking, other possibilities opened up that I had not seen before.

So now, in this classroom, in my sphere of influence, I work to hook children first of all into the idea that they are learners, and we develop a shared picture of what good learners do, how good learners behave. I try to let them know that I'm a learner with them, to share the things I'm learning. I try to plant the seeds that we're not learning in little boxes, we're learning together. I do a lot of modeling of behavior and of guiding them: "Ask your neighbor for help," or "Would you be willing to assist someone?"

I did not understand the dynamic learning that can go on when everyone in a classroom is both a learner and a teacher. Until I saw it in action. It's not easy to really explain unless you've experienced it. But that's what brings me back to work every day, because it is really very energizing to be part of this kind of thinking.

SOME POINTS TO CONSIDER

✔ Dawn, like Laurel, has found that giving children more responsibility results in a more productive classroom.

✔ For Dawn, the important difference was the shift she made in her role as instructional leader. Dawn was willing to experiment with a facilitative approach, even though as she says, "I did not understand the dynamic learning that can go on. . . . Until I saw it in action."

 Finding Your Philosophy

Laura Ecken's journey began with the idea that she would help children learn more about each other and develop a feeling of classroom community. She wasn't prepared for the profound discoveries that emerged from that seemingly simple, initial goal.

LAURA   When I started out that first year to try to build community, I listed it in my plan book for forty-five minutes a day, from 1:00 to 1:45. It sounds embarrassing now, but I really thought it was something that you could write in your plan book for a certain time.

It just dawned on me gradually that this way of working with kids is a philosophy that permeates your whole way of teaching and living, even your way of dealing with your family.

I guess before that I'd never really thought about what I was trying to accomplish in the classroom. I had a curriculum and I went in and taught it. I know it sounds really ignorant. But it had never occurred to me that I was trying to build a love of learning and a strong respect for other human beings. Once I thought about those goals I could see I wasn't working toward them. I had never realized that they were my goals. I had never thought, "Why are you here? What are you trying to accomplish?"

The year I first started doing relationship-building activities in the classroom, I really got to know the kids. I had never gotten to know them so well and so quickly before, and they got to know me. At the same time, things were very hectic that first month in my classroom. Instead of just putting names on the board when kids were doing something wrong, I constantly had to be talking to people about what they were doing. But suddenly it became obvious to me that there was no more humiliation in my classroom, no more manipulation of the students by threats, no more punishments at the end of the day.

I found my class was noisier. But I looked at how the students were talking to each other and how they were learning, and I realized it was something that they needed. Here were kids who were talking to each other eagerly, and mostly about school.

I also began to realize that this way would take longer and that I had to allow children time to learn to operate in ways that were new for them, too. Many of them were used to being *told* what to do, rather than being encouraged to make decisions and think for themselves.

I grew as the children did. I began to trust myself more and the learning the kids were doing. I began to take more account of what they were interested in, to have them ask their own questions, and to connect more of the curriculum to their lives.

I had never really thought about learning issues: Why do you want to do this in the classroom? What do you want kids to learn? What do you expect kids to do to get there? Once I did, I began to see, for example, that we didn't need to teach writing and reading in separate forty-minute periods. If we were doing a role-play from a reading lesson, I wouldn't worry about it lasting for two hours because kids were learning all sorts of skills—perspective-taking, writing, reading—all in the context of this rich work.

It all fits. Today, I said to the kids that we were going to change partners for literature, because they've done several books with the same partner, and they started cheering. I asked them about that, and someone said that it was fun to get to know new people and to find out about their families and their activities.

Then we had a discussion about how we treat people when we get new partners. Someone mentioned how hurtful it would be to say that they didn't want to work with someone or act like they didn't want to work with someone. Then another little boy said, "How would you know you wouldn't want to work with someone before you even get to know them?" Another student brought up a book we read at the beginning of the year, *Miss Maggie*, and said, "Nat thought he didn't like Miss Maggie because she was spitting tobacco and had a snake, but then he found out he did—and we could have experiences like that."

If the people in all of Louisville got to the point that the kids in my class are at, it would change Louisville. There would be no gangs. Those are the outcasts, the kids who find a sense of belonging in gangs. No child is left out in this school. There is no child who doesn't belong.

While we have many poor kids at Hazelwood, we don't have the problems they have in some middle-class schools. The substitutes always have a good day at Hazelwood. "There isn't any place like this school," a substitute said to me recently. We treat every child with respect. We give everyone the opportunity to learn and teach them to love to learn.

What all this has done for me is to help me to think about who I am as a teacher, what I'm doing, and why I do what I do. Once you've begun to think, really think about what you do, you can't go back to old ways. And once you've seen what being part of a caring learning community does for children, you wouldn't want to.

Resources

MOTIVATION AND LEARNING THEORY: AN OVERVIEW

COMMUNITY-BUILDING IDEAS TO TRY

COLLABORATIVE ACTIVITY CHECKLIST

EXCERPTS FROM *Blueprints for a Collaborative Classroom*

ANNOTATED BIBLIOGRAPHY OF ADDITIONAL RESOURCES

Motivation and Learning Theory: An Overview

THE TEACHERS who have opened to us their classrooms, teaching practices, and thinking have in common many beliefs about the goals of schooling and about how children learn and develop. For some, these beliefs are new—the result of a personal process of change that was supported or even initiated by their involvement with the Child Development Project. For others, these beliefs were already in place—and reflected in their classrooms—years ago.

The Behaviorist versus the Biological Perspective

I N THEIR thinking and practice, all the teachers in this book demonstrate what might be called a "biological perspective" on human behavior—although it is not a term most of them would use. A biological perspective assumes that the forces of natural selection shape everyone—including children—to have the characteristics necessary for survival in their environment: that is, children are deeply programmed to survive as individuals and to contribute to the survival of our social group.

A biological perspective stands in sharp contrast to behaviorism—the predominant influence in American education for the past thirty years—since behaviorism assumes that children are passive, blank slates, not deeply programmed survivors and contributors.

The implications of these two perspectives for how we teach can be put starkly: given a biological perspective, we *work with* children; given a behaviorist perspective, we *act on* them. From a biological perspective power is *internal*; from a behaviorist perspective, power is *external*.

Although a biological perspective has for decades been shaping the work of many developmental psychologists as well as European and European-influenced educators, it has only recently begun to compete with behaviorism in having an important influence in American education. The following brief review of the research that applies to the behaviorist and biological perspectives in education explains how behaviorism came to have such a stranglehold on American education, and why educators are increasingly abandoning it for a biological perspective.

Searching for the "Physics" of Behavior

As a theoretical perspective, behaviorism took its cues from what for many is the queen of the sciences—physics. Just as laws in physics are universal—applicable to all physical bodies equally whether the body is steel, marble, or wood, for example—so psychologists hoped to find universal laws that applied equally to all behaving organisms, whether they were rats, polar bears, or people.

The behaviorists—beginning early in the twentieth century with the Russian Ivan Pavlov and his salivating dogs and then following the lead of Americans E. L. Thorndike, J. B. Watson, and B. F. Skinner—assumed that all living organisms were oriented to satisfy a few primary drives: food, water, safety, and sex. Except for these primary drives, or primary reinforcers, all organisms were assumed to be "blank slates" that would change as a result of stimuli from the outside world. Furthermore, the behaviorists assumed that the laws for associating stimuli with responses in one organism would hold for all organisms—again, whether they were rats, polar bears, or people.

The behaviorist way to get any behaving organism to "learn" or perform a behavior (that it is capable of performing) is essentially a rewards system. When the organism exhibits the desired behavior or a close approximation, then a pleasant consequence follows—usually a primary reinforcer such as food, or some stimulus (such as praise) that had previously been paired with a primary reinforcer. This reinforcement pattern continues until the organism learns or begins performing the desired behavior more frequently. In this way dogs can be taught to sit, horses to walk on their hind legs, and children to say please.

These procedures were widely reported and imitated, leading not only to better animal acts in circuses but to behavioristic systems, such as token economies, for managing the behavior of institutionalized children and adults. It wasn't long until the principles of behaviorism were applied to the field of special education and then to classroom instruction in general.

Behaviorism Applied to Education

The initial success of behaviorist experiments boosted interest in finding "scientific" approaches to teaching complex behaviors, such as reading and mathematics. Behaviorist approaches were developed to replace the more holistic, intuitive, and eclectic approaches that teachers had been using for years. The new basal textbooks, for example, led teachers day-by-day and script-by-script through the teaching of reading so that students would experience the "scientific" sequence of learning to read. Teachers focused on one desired behavior at a time and praised or rewarded successive approximations until the desired behavior was acquired. They continued to reward the behavior until it was "overlearned"—until the particular association was so strong that the child would be unlikely to forget it.

In the blank slate, behaviorist paradigm, learning was simply the act of forming associations. Thus, associations—between letters and sounds, between dates and battles, between mathematical problems and the formulae for solving them—became the goal in all kinds of learning contexts.

Correspondingly, there arose a proliferation of systems of classroom management designed to scientifically control and shape students' behavior. Based on behaviorist principles, such systems taught teachers to ignore behavior they wanted children to stop doing and to reward desired behavior with praise, stickers, stars, points, and other such positive stimuli. Schools held auctions where students could buy material rewards with school "dollars" they had earned for good behavior; school staffs were encouraged to reward children with praise slips if they were "caught" being good.

Eventually, the rewards recommended by the behaviorists for positive behavior were supplemented with ways to address rather than avoid or ignore "mistakes." Schools instituted "time-out" chairs and even time-out rooms. Assertive Discipline (Cantor 1976), perhaps the most famous and influential of the classroom management systems based on behaviorism, instructed teachers to take marbles out of the jar as well as put them in; the checks on the board next to children's names were no longer to accumulate toward a material reward but to warn children how close they were to the next level of negative reinforcement. Assertive Discipline promised powerful short-term results and became so widespread that some school districts mandated its use and only interviewed teachers already trained to use it.

While the aggressive use of Assertive Discipline has faded, the behaviorist model of children as blank slates manipulated by rewards and punishments is still pervasive. Most of us, as teachers and as parents, have used it—whether our goal was for children to memorize spelling lists, learn about gravity, or make their beds. But as we will see below, some very important research discredits behaviorism as a means for teaching anything except arbitrary associations, such as those between a sugar cube and standing on one's hind legs, or between 1812 and a certain war.

Challenges to Behaviorism

As research psychologists working from the perspective of behaviorism expanded their study of animal learning, they began to find that the animals they were studying behaved in ways that defied the laws of behaviorism.

In ground-breaking experiments designed by John Garcia and his colleagues (1966a), rats were caused to fall sick some time after receiving a stimulus. When the stimulus was unusual tasting water, the rats learned to associate getting sick with the water. When the stimulus was a bright light and a noise, the rats did not learn to associate the stimulus with getting sick, although according to the laws of behaviorism they should have—either stimulus should have been as easy to learn to associate with getting sick as the other. Instead, as Garcia suggests, the rats in his experiment were somehow predisposed to think, "It must have been something I ate."

In a second, parallel study by Garcia and his colleagues (1966b), the rats readily associated receiving a shock to their paws with the bright light and noise but not with the unusual taste. It appears that rats are somehow prepared by the forces of natural selection to associate surface pain with audio-visual stimuli but not with tastes. Several years later, Hardy Wilcoxon and his colleagues (1971) found that quails, a species that relies mostly on visual cues for food detection, were more likely to associate getting sick with a color—or visual—stimulus than with a taste stimulus.

Biologically prepared rather than arbitrary response-stimulus associations seemed to be at work—the behaviorists themselves were finding evidence that led away from a "physics" of animal behavior and back toward a . . ."biology" of animal behavior.

The Contribution of Ethology

Beginning in the 1930s, European ethologists such as Nikko Tinbergen and Konrad Lorenz, in their work to understand animal behavior from a biological perspective, began documenting numerous ways in which animals were specially prepared to survive in their natural habitats. Ethologists studied a wide variety of species with the goal of understanding *instinct*, a full range of inbuilt or biologically prepared behavior, which American behaviorists had assumed did not exist beyond the very primitive drives for food, water, safety, and sex.

As ethologists documented the presence of complex instinctual behaviors, such as the tendency of baby ducks to follow their mothers or of mother gulls to recognize their chicks but not their eggs, it became more and more apparent that the processes of natural selection prepared animals with inbuilt *behavioral* characteristics that give them a survival advantage in their natural environment. As the British ethologist Aubrey Manning states, "Nearly all the behaviour we observe in animals is adaptive. They respond to appropriate stimuli in an effective manner . . . . Animals are not infallible, but when they do make mistakes it is often because they have been transported into an unnatural environment" (Manning 1972).

While the early success of studies in behaviorism had delayed Americans' serious consideration of the work of the European ethologists, the ethologists' biological perspective generated more interest once cracks appeared in behaviorist theory. Given the results of Garcia's and others' animal experiments combined with the ethologists' observations of biologically prepared behavior or instinct, the behaviorist metaphor of the blank slate was untenable: at the very least, each slate arrived with quite a bit of writing already on it.

In their book *Biological Boundaries of Learning*, Martin Seligman and Joanne Hager characterize this transition—the replacement of the blank slate with the acceptance of biological preparedness—as the beginning of a "scientific revolution" in the study of animal behavior. Rather than look outside the organism, as they had for external stimuli, scientists began to look inside the organism—as Jean Piaget had been doing in the field of human cognition for years.

Piaget and the Differentiation of Humans from Rats and Polar Bears

Observing humans rather than other animals, Jean Piaget and his colleagues began during the 1930s in Europe to document thought processes unique to human infants and children. These thought processes could not be explained on the basis of stimulus-response pairs, whether the pairs were the arbitrary ones predicted by the behaviorists or the biologically prepared ones observed by the ethologists. Instead, from his study of children Piaget described an entirely new kind of learning—a developmental progression from naive to increasingly more logical beliefs or theories about the nature of the physical and social world.

Since these naive beliefs or theories appear to occur to children universally and are not held by the adults in the children's environments, they cannot be the result of learning associations taught by adults. For example, children hold a coherent set of beliefs about consciousness that Piaget called "animism." With no apparent instruction, children between the ages of approximately four and seven attribute consciousness to all things, then shift to attributing consciousness only to things that move, then only to things that move of their own accord, and finally, around the age of eleven or twelve children restrict the attribution of consciousness to animals (Piaget [1929] 1969).

While the existence of such naive or childish beliefs clearly does not fit the metaphor of the blank slate, it also doesn't fit the metaphor of the slate with biologically prepared writing on it. What Piaget documented was that as children develop and interact with their environment, their beliefs about the world change over time *as a result of their own mental processes.* What appears to be biologically prepared in humans is more than a readiness to make certain associations—we appear to be biologically prepared for an additional kind of learning that involves constructing logical theories about the world. Piaget called this uniquely human form of learning "intelligence"; others have called it "understanding" or "cognition."

A Paradigm Shift in the Education of Children

THE CONCEPT of biological preparedness implies that living organisms are not just prepared, they are prepared for the particular environment in which they have evolved—"the environment of evolutionary adaptiveness" (Bowlby 1969). The *human* environment of evolutionary adaptiveness, in other words, both contributes to and reflects *humans'* particular physical, cognitive, and social needs. As Piaget discovered, human cognitive needs include the need to build theories and construct knowledge. Human social needs lead us to maintain a complex set of social systems—from family and peer groups to educational, economic, cultural, and political systems. It is the combination of these human cognitive and social needs that we, as educators, are committed to address.

Learning and Motivation from a Biological Perspective

From a biological perspective, it follows that if we want to better understand how to help *children* learn and contribute to their social group, we need to better understand the nature of *children*. We cannot generalize from what we know about the learning of rats or polar bears—and because humans go through fundamental changes as they develop, we also cannot generalize from what we know about the learning of human adults. Instead we can only optimize our efforts to help children learn and grow by understanding how they learn and develop, what they need in order to successfully develop, and how they affect and are affected by the social systems that are part of their natural environment.

This biological approach has profound implications for understanding children's motivation to learn, as well as their capacity to learn. We cannot assume, as the behaviorists did, that children are intrinsically motivated only to satisfy basic physical needs; nor is it sufficient to add social approval as a motivator (a move that distinguishes social learning theorists from classical behaviorists). Children have much to learn in order to master their environment, and they must master their environment in order to survive: therefore, from a biological perspective, we would expect children to be curious and innately interested in learning that which is relevant to their lives (even when their efforts are not reinforced by candy, stickers, or praise). Likewise, we would *not* assume that children have to be enticed or coerced to learn unless, of course, the learning was arbitrary and was perceived by the children as arbitrary. Teaching would be seen as helping children learn what they need and want to know—an enabling or facilitating process—in contrast to a coercive or controlling process.

These implications for understanding children's motivations are not limited to the realm of academic learning—they also apply to social and ethical learning. Since children must be cared for in order to survive, and since humans have evolved as part of social groups, a biological perspective would lead us to expect children to be intrinsically motivated to bond with their caretakers and to fit in with their social group. Biologically speaking, the processes of natural selection have prepared children to be receptive to the socializing influences of their caretakers and their social group. So, if children are biologically prepared to be part of their social group, then socializing children is also best seen as an enabling process—one of helping rather than coercing them to learn and live by the norms and values of society.

A biological perspective would lead us to expect children to be intrinsically motivated to bond with their caretakers and to fit in with their social group. Socializing children, then, is best seen as an enabling rather than a coercive process.

With regard to both capacity and motivation, human infants are born uniquely prepared to fit into, learn, and thrive in their natural environment. Thus, the role of adults in that environment is not to force development through external shaping, but to *guide and work with the child's natural tendencies to develop in an adaptive or positive direction.* We believe this is what Piaget meant when he said that all development is positive.

Research and Theory Embedded in the Child Development Project

A S EDUCATIONAL psychologists and researchers have shifted to a biological perspective, numerous approaches have arisen to understanding the nature of children, how they form relationships, how they learn and develop, what they need, and how they respond to the various environments in which they exist and learn. We will briefly summarize the several bodies of theory and research that have been most helpful in our efforts to design educational approaches aimed at fostering children's social, ethical, and intellectual development.

Motivation Theory: The ABCs of Intrinsic Motivation

If optimal learning depends on meeting children's biologically driven needs, it is important to know what those needs are. The three primary needs that have been identified (by different researchers working to describe intrinsic motivation on one hand and to describe attachment needs on the other) are easily remembered as the ABCs of intrinsic motivation: Autonomy, Belonging, and Competence. Autonomy can be described as the need to be in control of oneself or to act on the basis of free will (de Charms 1968); the need for belonging, or to feel accepted by and worthy of the care of others, has been well documented in the work spearheaded by John Bowlby in the development of attachment theory; and the third basic need, competence, is the need to be effective or to accomplish things (White 1959).

Edward Deci and Richard Ryan and their colleagues (1991) have developed a considerable body of research that strongly supports the idea that humans organize their behavior to satisfy all three needs—for autonomy, belonging, and competence. These researchers argue that when children are in an environment where they can satisfy the three needs, then they will be intrinsically motivated to learn what is important to learn in that environment. Likewise, children's motivation is undermined to the degree to which any of these conditions is not met.

The implications for a school setting, then, are to satisfy all three needs in creating a classroom environment and in designing learning tasks. The first condition that helps meet those needs—creating a caring classroom environment—is best understood in terms of attachment theory.

Children's Psychological Need for Belonging

In the late 1950s and early 1960s, John Bowlby began applying a biological perspective to understanding the mother-child relationship. He assumed that since mothers are essential to the survival of infants, infants should be biologically prepared to maintain closeness to their mothers or primary caretakers.

Through observations of infants in many parts of the world, Bowlby and others, most notably Mary Ainsworth (1964, 1967), established that when infants are separated from their mother they display various different behaviors depending on the basic quality of their relationship with her. From these observations, Bowlby developed attachment theory, which describes the psychological need for human closeness or belonging and the capacity to love and trust.

According to attachment theory, infants and children develop varying beliefs about their self-worth and the trustworthiness of others depending on how sensitively primary caretakers respond to their needs—including needs for playfulness and psychological close-ness. Infants and children with responsive caretakers will, Bowlby offered, develop beliefs that they are worthy of care and that they can trust that they will receive the care they need. On the other hand, infants with unresponsive caretakers will come to believe that they are unworthy of care and that they cannot trust that they will receive the care they need. These beliefs, it follows, will affect children's ability to act on their natural instinct—their biological preparedness—for empathic and cooperative relationships with others.

In fact, numerous researchers have documented how infants' and children's attachment relationships affect their social and ethical development. For example, children with histories of secure attachment relationships have been found to be more socially and empathically responsive (Main and Weston 1981), more cooperative with or obedient to their parent (Staton, Hogan, and Ainsworth 1971), and more competent with peers, more positive, more empathic, more likely to develop friendships, and less likely to victimize others (Sroufe 1983, 1988). Conversely, children with histories of unresponsive or hurtful parenting tend to behave in antisocial or maladaptive ways—for example, by being aggressive, or withdrawn and helpless, or overly compliant (Main and Weston 1981, Sroufe 1983, 1988).

Although attachment theory began by focusing on the mother-child relationship, it soon evolved to include other significant caretakers and therefore has implications for how we relate to children in the classroom—especially children whose beliefs about their self-worth and the trustworthiness of others have developed in negative ways. As Bowlby describes it, children carry their "inner working models" of themselves and others into any new social situation, where these models then shape their goals, behavior, expectations, and percep-tions.

Because, as both Piaget and Bowlby suggest, children are theory builders, one of our jobs as teachers is to help children build theories of themselves as worthy and of others as trust-worthy. Attachment theorists in particular argue for the importance of building dependable, supportive relationships with children and accompanying this support with high maturity demands. In these ways, we can build relationships with children that help change, if nec-essary, their theories about themselves and others and also help satisfy their basic need to belong.

In our work in the Child Development Project, we carried the concept of attachment into the classroom and conducted research that has documented its importance (Battistich et al. 1995). In six school districts, we found that when elementary school students experi-ence their schools and classrooms as caring communities—places where they feel they have some influence or control over their own behavior and where others care about and are responsive to their needs—they are also more likely to like school, trust and respect their teachers, enjoy challenging learning activities, be concerned about and help others, and resolve conflicts fairly and without force. Similarly, Anthony Bryk and Mary Driscoll (1988) found that high school students had higher interest in schooling, gains in mathematics achievement, better attendance, and lower dropout rates when their schools functioned as communities with shared values, common activities, and personalized, caring relationships among members.

These research findings are fully consistent with what we would expect, given a biological perspective on socialization—they describe the benefits of school environments where children experience belonging. The CDP findings also point to the importance of school environments where children experience autonomy—where they feel they have some influence or control over their life at school.

Children's Psychological Need for Autonomy

While the CDP study points to the positive effects of autonomy, much other research on children's autonomy describes the flip side—the negative effects on children when they are over-controlled. Deci and Ryan found many instances in which children's motivation to do a task decreased when their sense of autonomy was diminished. For example, children in elementary classrooms where their teachers had controlling styles reported less intrinsic motivation for school learning than children in classrooms where teachers offered more choice, explained the reasons behind rules, and in general had a more autonomy-supporting style (Deci et al. 1981; Ryan and Grolneck 1984). In a nursery school setting, children's interest and creativity in painting declined when they were given rules about how they had to handle the paints, unless the rules were presented in a noncontrolling manner—for example, as a means to paint better by keeping colors from getting muddy (Koestner et al. 1984).

The most common way that children's autonomy is diminished in school situations is, of course, by controlling them with rewards and punishments. Deci and Ryan and many others have documented that the promise of reward or the threat of punishment undermines children's intrinsic motivation to perform interesting tasks and impedes their development of internalized motivation to do useful but uninteresting tasks. Similarly, in *Growing Up Creative*, Theresa Amabile reports on several studies in which the use of external controls such as rewards seemed to interfere with students' creativity. In one study, for example, elementary school children's storytelling and collage-making were less creative when the children agreed to do these activities in order to get a reward. In another study, high school students who were offered a reward wrote less creative stories than those not promised a reward.

Deci and Ryan and their colleagues explain that this negative effect of perceived control arises from the subjects' need to maintain their autonomy—either by performing the task with less effort or by withdrawing from the task when they can (Deci and Porac 1978; Deci et al. 1991). Similar self-protective behaviors have been documented when children's sense of competence is threatened, as described below.

Children's Psychological Need for Competence

Children's third basic psychological need, to feel competent, must also be accounted for in designing learning environments and activities. For example, in reviewing his own studies and those of others with regard to children's competence, John Nicholls (1989) reports a general decline in performance in highly competitive situations, especially by children who estimate their ability to be normatively below that of their peers. Also, when children are offered a choice of learning tasks, those who are worried about their competence choose learning tasks that are far too difficult to do successfully or far too easy to provide meaningful challenge.

Viewing children as biologically prepared to meet their psychological need for competence, Nicholls explains this pattern by arguing that when their competence is put in jeopardy, children have three rational ways to preserve their sense of competence: avoid the task altogether; choose an easy task where success is assured; or choose a very difficult task where failure is assured, but would not imply lack of ability because the task itself is so difficult. Thus, Nicholls advises, we should maximize the learning potential of all our students by presenting learning tasks in ways that do not heighten students' sense of normative standing—that focus students on what they can learn or accomplish, not on whether they are as good as or better than others.

In summary, the implications of motivational theory and research are fully consistent with a biological perspective on human learning: from that perspective we would expect children (indeed all humans) to be intrinsically motivated to learn or engage in tasks that meet their needs, but when tasks or situations have conflicting effects on these needs, to try to alter or escape from such situations. Thus, if we want to foster students' motivation to learn what we are charged with teaching, we will design learning environments and learning tasks that maximize students' potential for satisfying their biologically-based needs for autonomy, belonging, and competence. When that is accomplished, children will be our willing collaborators as we help them learn what they need to be thoughtful and productive members of their social group.

Cognitive Theory: The Development of Understanding

The biological perspective has implications for how we think about the *nature* of learning as well as for how we design motivating learning tasks and environments. If our goal is to foster students' cognition—something quite different from fostering the associations implicit in behaviorism—then we need to understand the nature of cognition and how to support its growth and development.

As mentioned earlier, the revolutionary work of Piaget and others studying children's cognitive development led to the description of a uniquely human form of learning—the building of logically coherent mental representations, or theories, about the nature of the physical and social world. Constance Kamii and others (1984, 1985) further specified that these theories must represent "autonomous" thinking—that is, believing in your mental structures or theories because they make sense to you, not because someone has told you to believe them. The purpose of such theory building, as Rheta DeVries and Betty Zan (1996) and others have argued, is not simply to construct personal understanding of the world, but to construct understanding that leads to the maintenance of the social group—through cooperation with others in ways that are just. Understanding the world and cooperating with others are the tasks required for survival, the tasks for which humans are biologically prepared. It follows, then, that teaching and learning should be designed to support such purposes.

In addition to Kamii and DeVries, numerous educators have drawn implications for such educational practice from Piaget's work. The work we describe below of Irving Sigel and his colleagues (1970, 1977, 1979) focuses on how young children develop the capacity for autonomous thinking.

Developing Understanding in Young Children

In studying young children (ages two to five), Sigel found that those who could not build abstract mental representations were hampered in their ability to solve various cognitive tasks. For example, some children were able to perform classification tasks with concrete objects but not with pictures of objects. Sigel labeled children's ability to build mental representations that are logical, coherent, and consistent with reality "representational competence" and equated it with their ability to develop an understanding of the world.

In the introduction to *Educating the Young Thinker*, Sigel summarizes his research over a number of years and describes the educational practices he and his colleagues developed to foster preschool children's thinking. In general Sigel suggests that representational competence is fostered when children are encouraged "to think for themselves, to appreciate options in solving problems, to understand that ideas can be represented in many forms, and to represent mentally non-present situations, objects, and events."

Through the constant process of adjusting and refining their thinking to account for discrepancies between their current mental representations and reality, children build not only their understanding, but their capacity to understand.

Sigel also argues that children need to be encouraged to confront discrepancies between their current mental representations, or understandings, and reality. It is through this constant process of adjusting and refining their thinking to account for discrepancies that children build not only their understanding, but also their capacity to understand.

To apply Sigel's work in the classroom, we would want to create a learning environment that encourages children to build their own mental representations—to think for themselves—and we would also want to provide a learning environment in which children have the confidence to confront the inaccuracies of their thinking and adjust their beliefs accordingly. Such a learning environment is both challenging and supportive: if it is not challenging, students will not see the need to change their naive and inaccurate ideas; if it is not supportive, they will not have the courage to risk being wrong—and thus the courage to think for themselves. Sigel's work suggests that to teach for understanding, we must constantly encourage our students to be mentally flexible, to risk thinking for themselves, and to go beyond that of which they are sure, while we simultaneously provide a supportive atmosphere in which they can trust that they will not be humiliated or embarrassed by their attempts to understand and communicate their thinking to others.

Developing Understanding in Adolescents and Youth

Howard Gardner's work complements Sigel's, with a focus on older students and their need to replace inaccurate naive theories with the coherent theories that have been generated in such disciplines as mathematics, science, and philosophy over the last two thousand or so years.

In *The Unschooled Mind*, Gardner argues that at least two conditions make it difficult for older students to develop the complex forms of thought (or in Piaget's terms, "formal operations") that make it possible to develop genuine understanding of the complex bodies of discipline knowledge. These negative conditions include a lack of theory-building experiences in the primary grades, as well as current teaching practices that primarily entail telling students what to remember. Given these conditions, older students hold onto their incorrect but powerful naive theories and add the incompatible set of memorized—but not understood—facts, concepts, and theories we are trying to teach them.

For example, a child who has "learned" probability theory simply by memorizing the correct formulas will quickly revert to or may simultaneously hold the naive belief that after a coin has come up heads several times in a row, it is more likely to come up tails on the next toss (so common is this naive belief that it has a name—"gambler's fallacy"). In another example, Gardner and his colleagues studied the quality of high school students' learning about complex concepts such as density. They found that large numbers of students quickly forgot the meaning of these concepts, even though they had been able to define them accurately and use what they had learned to solve problems on tests. He suggests that they forgot because they never really understood the concepts when they "learned" them.

In preschool and elementary school, concrete experience can help children refine their theories; for example, the child tossing coins could replace the naive "gambler's fallacy" with an accurate understanding of probability by tallying the results of many, many consecutive coin tosses, combining his or her tosses with those of classmates, and creating a theory that accounts for all the collected data. If children are accustomed to doing the hard work of thinking for themselves and readjusting or revising their thinking when it does not fit reality, then they will be prepared when they reach middle school and high school to undertake the difficult work of mastering the approaches, abstract theories, and complex bodies of knowledge that comprise the different disciplines.

However, given the complexity of the discipline knowledge that middle school and high school students encounter, it is not reasonable to expect them to understand it by inventing or reinventing theories in the same way younger students do. At this stage it is important to *provide* students with theories—but not in their full complexity, and not without giving them concrete ways to work with the theories. As Marcia Linn and Lawrence

Muilenburg (1996) argue with regard to science education, the approach we take with adolescents should present them with increasingly more complex and accurate theories and give them lots of opportunities to apply those theories to concrete, ordinary events in their lives. The goal is to help them "have a generative understanding and an inclination to progressively refine their ideas"—in other words, to set them on a course of lifelong learning.

Howard Gardner and Veronica Boix-Mansilla (1989) make a similar point, demonstrating the broad applications of generative learning: "It does not benefit the rookie pianist to hear Arthur Rubinstein or the novice tennis player only to witness Martina Navratilova. Rather, students must encounter individual benchmarks on the trail from novice to expert, as well as road maps of how to get from one milestone to the next. Given these landmarks, along with ample opportunity to perform their understanding with appropriate feedback, most individuals should be able to steadily enhance their competence in any discipline."

Obviously, it takes more time to garner these concrete experiences and go through the difficult process of building new mental representations and eliminating old ones than it does to memorize a set of problem-solving strategies or formulas—yet the amount of time we feel comfortable providing for such learning seems to decrease as children move up the grades. Whether the pressure to hurry children along comes from an ever-expanding curriculum, assessment systems that measure memory rather than understanding, or a pedagogy based on behaviorist learning principles, we typically do not take the time required for our students to build their own mental representations and to think for themselves.

But as Sigel and Gardner would agree, whether learners are in preschool or high school, the necessary conditions for learning for understanding are the same: support, challenge, and time. These conditions are further elaborated in the work of the sociocultural theorists described below.

A Sociocultural Lens on Understanding

At about the same time that Jean Piaget was focusing on how children develop the capacity for logical thought, Lev Vygotsky was focusing on a quite different aspect of cognition: how humans acquire the skills and knowledge of their culture. Both researchers worked from a biological perspective, but Piaget investigated children's theory building in response to their *individual* interactions with the environment. Vygotsky viewed children as inseparable from their social system and their culture. His concern with how culture shapes human thought has been called a sociocultural or sociohistorical perspective on human learning (Rogoff 1990).

In sociocultural theory, as in Piagetian theory, knowledge is something which must be constructed, but Vygotsky stressed the social nature of this construction and the role of "more knowledgeable others" in helping children acquire the skills and knowledge that a society has developed over the years. Vygotsky and others working from this perspective see adults or more accomplished members of the culture as biologically prepared to assist or "scaffold" children's learning; they see children as biologically prepared to benefit from such a relationship—to abstract the knowledge and acquire the skills of their culture as they observe and work with the culture's more knowledgeable others.

Barbara Rogoff takes this view one step further by arguing that children are biologically programmed not only to accept but to *seek* the social support they need to learn the skills of their culture, in much the same way an apprentice seeks the support of a master craftsman. In *Apprenticeship in Thinking: Cognitive Development in Social Context*, she documents numerous examples from the United States and Mayan cultures of children's active solicitation of support for their learning from adults or older children in informal learning situations. She also provides evidence of the facilitative effect of adult "guided participation" on children's learning: for example, when adults collaborated with children in planning an efficient route for accomplishing a series of errands, the children were later found to be more able to complete a similar task on their own.

In summarizing her own theory and research, as well as that of Vygotsky and others working within the context of sociocultural theory, Rogoff stresses that the learning process requires that adults *gradually* transfer responsibility to children while offering "adjusted support that provides both challenge and sensitive assistance. The freedom to err in manageable (or even graceful) ways is inherent to a transfer of responsibility," she concludes.

The sociocultural theorists have documented learning that occurs not through direct instruction motivated by the promise of reward, but through joint activity with a shared goal. In these learning activities children are seeking adult guidance, but the motivation for the learning springs naturally from children's desire to become adults—productive and competent members of their culture. While we have much to learn about the conditions that maximize children's learning, whether in collaboration with peers or with adults, the work of researchers in sociocultural theory clearly supports the biological view that children are naturally motivated to learn that which they see as relevant to productive adult life in their culture. Thus, if we want to foster students' intrinsic motivation to learn, we will help them see that the learning is relevant to understanding the physical or social world, or to productive participation in their culture.

Another important implication of sociocultural theory for education is that through the many informal interactions children have with the adults in their families and communities, they will have already learned—prior ever to coming to school—what is "important" to learn and how to learn. Therefore, we would expect that if the values and style of adult-child interaction in the child's home culture are quite different from those of the school culture, the child will have a difficult time adjusting to school learning experiences. Roland Tharp (1989), reviewing numerous studies of the school performance of children whose home cultures were substantially different from the school cultural, concludes that such a disjuncture does, in fact, disadvantage children.

Furthermore, if the child brings to school a quite different body of knowledge and set of experiences from the teacher's, the apprenticeship relationship will suffer. The teacher will not recognize the child's goals, full range of competencies, or areas ripe for development, and will thus be unable to sensitively challenge and assist the child's performance. Barbara Rogoff reports research by Michaels and Cazden (1986), for example, in which African American and white teachers read anonymous transcripts of African American and white children's sharing-time narratives. The narratives had no group identifying characteristics, yet the teachers from each racial group unwittingly credited the children from the other, less familiar group, with less competence than the children whose backgrounds matched their own.

It follows from sociocultural theory and research, then, that if we are to educate all children we need to understand their home cultures. We will want to adjust our teaching strategies and goals to incorporate and honor what children bring to the classroom, as well as help children adjust or add to their learning strategies and goals those that are valued in the majority or school culture. This is a challenging goal in a multicultural society—to accomplish it we must reach out to and collaborate with each child's parents or guardians.

Summary

In reviewing the theories and research that make up our understanding of attachment, intrinsic motivation, cognition, and sociocultural transfer, several principles emerge in support of our understanding of a biological perspective on human learning and behavior:

- First, children are seen as adapting to the world around them in rational, self-protective ways. Thus, if we view their behaviors as rational, we will be better able to understand the causes and goals of any given behavior and better able to influence it positively.

- Second, children are seen as having distinct needs which they are biologically prepared to satisfy. Thus, if we understand these needs and the ways in which they are and are not being met, we can help children satisfy them in ways that are supportive of their development.

- Third, children's learning involves an active construction of theories about the world, and these theories undergo changes with children's development and experiences. For example, young children believe that things that move are alive and that things have to be equal to be fair; later on they develop more differentiated views of life and justice.

• Fourth, the human environment of evolutionary adaptiveness has an essentially social and communal/cooperative nature, which means that humans are biologically prepared to live and interact in ways that preserve their social relationships and their community.

• And finally, such a community—a supportive and challenging social environment—is essential for children's intellectual, social, and ethical development.

The theory guiding the development of the Child Development Project and the teaching practices described in this book is anchored in the biological view that children's development is a positive or adaptive process that requires a supportive and challenging social context. The ideas for how to apply this theoretical perspective in elementary schools and classrooms in order to foster children's social, ethical, and intellectual development have come from many sources—the experiences and thinking of the classroom teachers with whom we have worked, the thinking and research of numerous psychologists and educational researchers, and our own experiences, research, and observations.

We believe we have constructed a coherent theory of how to promote children's development in schools and classrooms. And like all good theory builders, we also understand the importance of continually confronting discrepancies in our theory and adjusting and refining it. We welcome your critical response.

List of References

Mary Ainsworth, "Patterns of Attachment Behaviour Shown by the Infant in Interaction with his Mother," *Merrill-Palmer Quarterly*, 10 (1964), 51–58.

Mary Ainsworth, *Infancy in Uganda: Infant Care and the Growth of Attachment* (The Johns Hopkins Press, 1967).

Theresa Amabile, *Growing Up Creative* (Crown, 1989).

Victor Battistich, Dan Solomon, Dong-il Kim, Marilyn Watson, and Eric Schaps, "Schools as Communities, Poverty Levels of Student Populations, and Students' Attitudes, Motives, and Performance: A Multilevel Analysis," *American Educational Research Journal*, 32 (1995), 627–658.

John Bowlby, *Attachment and Loss: Volume I: Attachment* (The Hogarth Press, 1969).

Anthony Bryk and Mary Driscoll, *The High School as Community: Contextual Influences, and Consequences for Students and Teachers* (National Center on Effective Secondary Schools, University of Wisconsin, 1988).

Lee Cantor, *Assertive Discipline: A Take-Charge Approach for Today's Educator* (Lee Cantor and Associates, 1976).

Carol Copple, Irving E. Sigel, and Ruth Saunders, *Educating the Young Thinker* (D. Van Nostrand Company, 1979).

Richard de Charms, *Personal Causation* (Plenum Press, 1968).

Edward Deci and Joseph Porac, "Cognitive Evaluation Theory and the Study of Human Motivation," in Mark R. Lepper and David Greene, eds., *The Hidden Costs of Reward: New Perspectives on the Psychology of Human Motivation* (Lawrence Erlbaum Associates, 1978).

Edward Deci, M. J. Schwartz, L. Sheinman, and Richard Ryan, "An Instrument to Assess Adults' Orientation toward Control Versus Autonomy with Children: Reflections on Intrinsic Motivation and Perceived Competence," *Journal of Educational Psychology*, 73 (1981), 642–650.

Edward Deci and Richard M. Ryan, "A Motivational Approach to Self: Integration in Personality" in R. Dienstbier, ed., *Nebraska Symposium on Motivation: Volume 38: Perspectives on Motivation* (University of Nebraska Press, 1991).

Edward L. Deci, Robert J. Vallerand, Luc G. Pelletier, and Richard M. Ryan, "Motivation and Education: The Self-Determination Perspective," *Educational Psychologist*, 26: 3 & 4 (1991), 325–346.

Rheta DeVries and Betty Zan, *Moral Classrooms, Moral Children: Creating a Constructivist Atmosphere in Early Education* (Teachers College Press, 1996).

John Garcia and Robert A. Koelling, "Relation of Cue to Consequence in Avoidance Learning," *Psychonomic Science*, 4 (1966a), 123–124.

John Garcia, Frank R. Ervin, and Robert A. Koelling, "Learning with Prolonged Delay of Reinforcement," *Psychonomic Science*, 5 (1966b), 121–122.

Howard Gardner, *The Unschooled Mind: How Children Think and How Schools Should Teach* (Basic Books, 1991).

Howard Gardner and Veronica Boix-Mansilla, "Teaching for Understanding–Within and Across the Disciplines," *Educational Leadership*, 51 (1989), 14–18.

Constance Kamii, "Obedience Is Not Enough," *Young Children* (May 1984), 11–14.

Constance Kamii, *Young Children Reinvent Arithmetic: Implications of Piaget's Theory* (Teachers College Press, 1985).

R. Koestner, R. Ryan, F. Bernieri, and K. Holt, "Setting Limits on Children's Behavior: The Differential Effects of Controlling vs. Informational Styles on Intrinsic Motivation and Creativity," *Journal of Personality*, 52 (1984), 233–48.

Marcia Linn and Lawrence Muilenburg, "Creating Lifelong Science Learners: What Models Form a Firm Foundation," *Educational Researcher*, 25 (1996), 18–24.

Mary Main and Donna Weston, "The Quality of the Toddler's Relationship to Mother and Father: Related to Conflict Behavior and the Readiness to Establish New Relationships," *Child Development*, 52 (1981), 932–940.

Aubrey Manning, "The Development of Behaviour" in Martin Seligman and Joanne Hager, eds., *Biological Boundaries of Learning* (Prentice-Hall, 1972).

S. Michaels and C. B. Cazden, "Teacher/Child Collaboration as Oral Preparation for Literacy" in B. B. Schieffelin and P. Gilmore, eds., *The Acquisition of Literacy: Ethnographic Perspectives* (Ablex, 1986).

John G. Nicholls, *The Competitive Ethos and Democratic Education* (Harvard University Press, 1989).

Jean Piaget, *The Child's Conception of the World*, Joan and Andrew Tomlinson, trans. (Littlefield, Adams & Company, 1969).

Barbara Rogoff, *Apprenticeship in Thinking: Cognitive Development in Social Context*, (Oxford University Press, 1990).

Richard Ryan and Wendy Grolneck, "Origins and Pawns in the Classroom: Self-Report and Projective Assessments of Individual Differences in Children's Perceptions," *Journal of Personality and Social Psychology*, 50 (1984), 550–558.

Martin Seligman and Joanne Hager, *Biological Boundaries of Learning* (Prentice Hall, Inc., 1972).

Irving E. Sigel, "The Distancing Hypothesis: A Causal Hypothesis for the Acquisition of Representational Thought," in M. R. Jones, ed., *The Effects of Early Experience* (University of Miami Press, 1970).

Irving E. Sigel and Rodney Cocking, *Cognitive Development from Childhood to Adolesence: A Constructivist Perspective* (Holt, Rinehart and Winston, 1977).

L. Alan Sroufe, "Infant-Caregiver Attachment and Patterns of Adaptation in the Preschool: The Roots of Competence and Maladaption" in M. Perlmutter, ed., *Minnesota Symposia in Child Psychology*, 16 (Lawrence Erlbaum Associates, 1983).

L. Alan Sroufe, "The Role of Infant-Caregiver Attachment in Development" in J. Belsky and T. Nezworski, eds., *Clinical Implications of Attachment* (Lawrence Erlbaum Associates, 1988).

D. Staton, R. Hogan and M. Ainsworth, "Infant Obedience and Maternal Behavior: The Origins of Socialization Reconsidered," *Child Development*, 42 (1971), 1057–1069.

Roland Tharp, "Psychocultural Variables and Constants: Effects on Teaching and Learning in Schools," *American Psychologist*, 44 (1989), 349–359.

Robert W. White, "Motivation Reconsidered: The Concept of Competence," *Psychological Review*, 60:5 (1959), 297–333.

Hardy Wilcoxon, William B. Dragoin, and Paul A. Kral, "Illness-Induced Aversions in Rat and Quail: Relative Salience of Visual and Gustatory Cues," *Science*, 171 (1971), 826–828.

Lev Vygotsky, *Thought and Language*, E. Haufman and G. Vakar, eds. and trans. (MIT Press, 1962).

Community-Building Ideas to Try

MANY COMMUNITY-building strategies, ideas, and activities are described throughout this book in various classroom spotlights and collegial conversations. Here, we include a further sampling of classroom-tested community-building ideas to use in the beginning of the year and whenever some getting-together or getting-to-know-you time is called for.

These activities are fun and of interest to children in and of themselves. Remember their purpose, though, and leave time after each activity to engage children in a process of reflection and discussion. For example, ask what they have learned from an activity, and have them reflect on how this helps them as a classroom community.

Building a Feeling of Class or Group Community

Class Web. With the class sitting in a circle, children, one at a time, hold a ball of yarn and introduce themselves by name and by telling something about themselves. Then, holding the end of the yarn, the children roll the ball across the circle to another class member, who continues the process. As children proceed, the ball unwinds into a web connecting everyone.

Adjective Alliteration. Children introduce themselves around a class circle, using their name and a positive adjective that starts with the same sound, for example, *marvelous* Marvin. This could also be done as a way for partners to introduce each other to the class, or as a game in which each child must include all previous introductions before making his or her own.

Class Name. Involve children in a process of selecting a class name (or motto, symbol, logo, etc.). Begin with a brainstorm, narrow the range of options, and seek consensus on the final choice.

Class Dragon. Have children each decorate a paper plate as they like. When the plates are strung together they make a class dragon to which every child has contributed. In a similar fashion, children can create a caterpillar, train, or any other such construction made up of segments or parts.

Class Quilt. On six-inch squares of paper students write their names and add whatever information, drawings, designs, or cut-outs they wish. For example, they could include pictures or information about their families, pets, or special interests as a way of sharing who they are. The squares are assembled to form a "quilt" in which each child (and the teacher) is represented by one patch.

Reading Aloud. Gather all of the children together to hear and discuss a story. At the beginning of the year, books that address issues such as making new friends or entering a new school can help children to reflect on and understand their experiences and feelings, and to enter their new environment more confidently and successfully.

Class History Collection. Keep track of memorable moments in the life of the class by having children collect mementos, photos, writings, drawings—anything that says "Here we are!" An ongoing timeline, scrapbook, bulletin board, and periodic newsletter are all possible ways for children to record their year together.

Building Friendships by Getting to Know One Another

Find Your Match. Children find and form groups with others in the class who share a particular attribute, such as the same birthday month. The group then explores other things they have in common, also discovering differences in the process. Groups can also be formed by interest—for example, by having children group themselves around their favorite animal picture or quotation and talk about why they chose that one.

People Collection. Plan a list of descriptions, each of which you know will be true of one or more people in the class, including yourself. Children then use the list to "collect" the names of classmates who fit into the categories. Without making the activity a competition, encourage children to get as many different names down on their list as possible. In this way, they will get to talk to lots of other people. The list might include descriptions such as the following:

1. Was born in another country
2. Is new to the school this year
3. Loves pizza
4. Knows a lot about Mexico

Partner Idea Lists. Partners take turns generating, listening to, and discussing one another's ideas on a given topic, such as: favorite books, things we want to learn about this year, people we admire.

Partner Interviews. Partners interview each other about a particular topic or interest, such as: things I'm proud of, what I'd like to contribute to our class this year, what I care about in a friend. They then write, draw, or tell others the information they have gained about their partner. Have children interview many different classmates early in the year.

Class Graphs and Data Bases. How many children have pets—how many have parakeets? guppies? dogs? snakes? How many children have siblings—how many brothers? sisters? How many children like to eat—ice cream? broccoli? banana slugs? Let children think up categories and record their findings in bar graphs, pie charts, and pictograms.

Special Person of the Week (SPOW). There are many variations on this activity, but one of the goals is to have every child get a turn over time to share special facts, photos, mementos, poems, drawings, family stories, or other information that is important to or about themselves.

Building Teacher-Child Relationships

Partner Interviews. Have a child interview the teacher as a model of the process for everyone. In this way, children can get to know their teacher, too.

Special Person of the Week (SPOW). Most teachers we know begin with themselves as a way of modeling this activity and letting children learn about their teacher as a person.

The Lunch Bunch. Children have lunch on one day of the week with the teacher. Participation is voluntary, and groups are kept very small and informal. One teacher we know takes two or three children at a time out for fast food on Fridays, and over the year all children have a turn.

Personal Stories. Children love to hear stories about their teacher's dog, children, spouse, childhood, disastrous trip to the grocery, favorite team, etc. Salt these stories into informal conversations with children and build them into introductions to academic activities in which children will also be drawing on a personal experience.

Collaborative Activity Checklist

NAME OF ACTIVITY: _____

ACADEMIC GOALS:_____

SOCIAL GOALS: _____

DATE OF DELIVERY: _____

Overall Design Considerations

✔ **Did children learn and accomplish more doing this activity as a group than they would have if they had done it alone?**

☐ Did the activity require children to make meaningful joint decisions?

☐ Did the activity require children to exchange ideas or points of view?

☐ Did the activity encourage children to help each other?

✔ **Was the activity open-ended enough for each group member to participate effectively?**

☐ Were there multiple tasks that utilized different strengths, talents, and skills?

☐ Did the activity provide opportunities for each child to both give and receive?

Activity Introduction

✔ **Did I make the importance and purpose of the activity clear?**

☐ Did I make it possible for children to see how the activity built from what they know or have experienced?

☐ Did I help children recognize how the activity was connected to their interests and concerns?

✔ **Did I make the learning task clear but not rigid?**

☐ Was I clear without overexplaining or overstructuring the task?

☐ Did I encourage children to clarify the task with each other?

☐ Did I model unfamiliar processes, as necessary, without limiting students' options?

✔ **Did I explain the social focus of the activity?**

☐ Did I help children think about why this was the focus?

✔ **Did I help children anticipate the social demands of the activity?**

☐ Did I help them rehearse, as necessary, related concrete behaviors and facilitative language?

☐ Did I model behavior and language, as necessary, without limiting their options?

Group Work

✔ **Were groups generally engaged in the learning task? If not . . .**

☐ Was my introduction insufficiently connected to students' interests or concerns?

☐ Were the directions confusing?

☐ Was the task too hard for many or all students?

☐ Was the task too easy for many or all students?

✔ **Were most groups reasonably successful working together? If not . . .**

☐ Was the task so challenging or so boring that it put unreasonable stress on students' social skills?

Teacher Observation of Groups

✔ Was I able to observe and monitor with a purposeful focus?

✔ Was I able to ask questions to scaffold learning or refocus children as necessary?

✔ Was I able to provide useful feedback as well as elicit students' self-assessments?

✔ Was I able to intervene in ways that foster student responsibility, thinking, and problem-solving?

Student Reflection

✔ **Were children comfortable articulating their academic learning and/or challenges?**

☐ Do they need more practice?

☐ Do they feel safe?

✔ **Were children comfortable articulating their social learning and/or challenges?**

☐ Do they need more practice?

☐ Do they feel safe?

✔ **Did my facilitation skills enable children to learn from and respond to the comments of others?**

☐ Did I ask open-ended questions?

☐ Did I ask questions that are hard to ignore, such as "How many others think that?" or "Who disagrees?" or "Is *this* or *that* or *that* more like what you think/learned/experienced?"

☐ Did I encourage children to speak directly to each other?

Teacher Analysis

✔ What did I learn about my students' academic strengths and challenges?

✔ What did I learn about my students' social strengths and challenges?

✔ What did I learn about the strengths and weaknesses of this activity?

✔ What did I learn about my own practice?

✔ How can I apply these learnings?

Excerpts from *Blueprints for a Collaborative Classroom*

THE FORMATS for partner and group work that follow, Interviewing and Poetry, are two of the twenty-five formats provided in *Blueprints for a Collaborative Classroom.* Several of the "Classroom Spotlights" in this book are built around such "blueprints" (see especially the partner interview activity "You Brought It in a Bag and Kept It a Secret" on page 22 and the group poetry activity "First We Talk" on page 107).

Interviewing

I NTERVIEWING their peers or adults is a great way for students to develop important communication skills while also learning about a subject, each other, or the world around them. Interviewing can be a particularly useful tool in building a collaborative classroom: students come to school with different experiences and knowledge, and interviews help them understand and benefit from each other's differences and perspectives. Use this flexible format as an interesting way for students to become engaged in a subject, to build interpersonal familiarity and respect, and to convey the message that students can learn from one another.

WHY TO USE

- to create and maintain a caring classroom community by helping students get to know each other
- to provide a relatively non-threatening way for partners to share ideas
- to show students that they can be learning resources for each other
- to engage students in a subject by helping them see how it connects to their own lives or the lives of others
- to help students develop important listening and communication skills

WHEN TO USE

- when students' or guests' personal perspectives and experiences can be injected into the study of a subject
- when a topic or issue is open-ended and students will benefit from hearing various perspectives
- when all students have personal knowledge or experience relevant to a topic
- when student presentations can be transformed from monologues into collaborative whole-class interactions

HOW TO DO

For partner interviews, the Interviewing format asks students to

- ask their partner questions about what they want to know
- check with their partner to make sure it's okay to share the information they got from the interview
- record their partner's information in writing, drawing, or orally
- check with their partner to make sure the report is accurate
- fix anything that's inaccurate and check again
- present their report about their partner to the class ▶

HOW TO DO For whole-class interviews, the Interviewing format asks students to

- ask the interviewee questions about what they want to know
- give classmates a chance to ask their questions, too!

Developmental Considerations

Younger students
Young children have their own ideas about what is significant and interesting—a characteristic that can be both charming and exasperating. In interviews, young children tend to zero in on specifics rather than abstractions—for example, the boys in the "Fly-on-the-Wall" vignette are far less concerned with discussing the topic of "helping" than they are with accurately representing the physical details of the situation! Accept and enjoy this window into students' thinking, and use whole-class wrap-ups to help students move beyond specifics and draw out larger concepts.

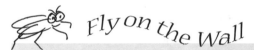

Fly on the Wall

In this first-grade class, the teacher has asked partners to interview each other and draw a picture about a time they helped someone. As Joey interviews Alfonso, he is careful to ask about details for his drawing and to check for accuracy with his partner.

JOEY: Who'd you help?

ALFONSO: I helped Scott, yesterday. Yesterday morning.

JOEY: And, um, how come?

ALFONSO: Because he fell down.

JOEY: And, um, where'd you take him?

ALFONSO: To the Yard Duty.

JOEY: Was it on cement or grass?

ALFONSO: Cement.

JOEY: Okeydokey. *(As he draws)* There's the cement. Now, how far

was it to the Yard Duty?

ALFONSO: Um, I don't quite remember...

JOEY: About this far? *(He shows Alfonso where he might draw it on the paper)*

ALFONSO: Yeah, that far—yeah, yeah.

JOEY: *(As he begins drawing Alfonso and Scott)* I think I'll just fill in their heads—kind of get a head start?

ALFONSO: Yeah, looks nice.

JOEY: *(Indicating the figure he's drawing)* That's you, and you're helping Scott—

ALFONSO: —and Scott's fell down.

JOEY: *(Drawing another figure)* Okay, this is Scott . . . . he has a smaller head than you. Now, what else do you want me to put in?

ALFONSO: (Looking over the drawing) Hmmm.

JOEY: Should I put the blue sky up?

ALFONSO: Yeah, blue sky. And that's it. *(Joey adds the sky)* Hey, why don't you put the office there?

JOEY: Hmmm, and maybe I should put the gate over here—

ALFONSO: Yeah, the gate!

JOEY: That's the gate . . . Are you finished?

ALFONSO: Uh, not quite yet—you know why? You need the soft ground next to the gate.

JOEY: Oh, I need the dirt—

ALFONSO: Yeah, the dirt!

JOEY: *(As he draws dots to indicate the dirt)* Speck, speck, speck, speck, speck, speck, speck—

ALFONSO: That's it. That's all you need to do. That's better!

JOEY: Finished?

ALFONSO: Yes, you're finished.

≈HINT≈

Many students are accustomed to answering questions and may have trouble asking and following up questions in ways that keep an interview going. Model these skills for them, explaining what you do, and give them lots of practice generating their own questions throughout the curriculum.

Also keep in mind that young children find it particularly difficult to report on their partners instead of themselves—they are far more inclined to tell their own story when it comes time to share with the whole class, because these are the details that are most memorable and immediate to them. (That's why activities involving tangible objects, such as Talking Artifacts on page xx, are exceptionally useful with young children—they have something concrete to keep their interview and their report on track.) Before their interviews, remind students to take care in recording their partner's story, and when necessary gently steer them back on course during their reports to the class. Of course, role-playing and modeling these skills will be prove even more effective than verbal reminders in the long run.

Finally, take the "communication" pressure off emergent writers by having them draw what they learn about their partners, as in the "Fly-on-the-Wall" vignette. Have children augment their drawings with dialogue or thought bubbles, or short captions, as unintimidating ways to engage their blossoming writing skills in interview activities.

Older students

Being more verbally skilled than young children, older students may find it difficult to trust someone else to accurately report their ideas. Encourage partners to collaborate closely so that they can adequately portray one another's thoughts and feelings; when necessary, review how to have accurate and respectful reports, such as suggested in Relinquishing Control on page xx.

Students of all ages (any of us, for that matter) will find their own ideas especially interesting and will have to work at listening as eagerly to others'. Older students, however, can more easily be made aware of this tendency and work toward becoming as involved and engaged in the interviewer role as in telling their own story. Challenge student interviewers to take responsibility for asking questions and making comments that help their partner think more deeply about the interview topic.

Grouping Considerations

Interviewing can be done in partnerships or as a whole class, depending upon whether one person has specialized information that the whole class can learn from or everyone has relevant information that can be profitably shared.

Each configuration serves other valuable objectives, as well. In partner interviews, students take turns interviewing each other and then present what they have learned about their partner to the class (via drawings, writing, collages, oral reports, etc.). In doing so they learn to listen attentively and present information clearly to others. Also, partner interviews offer shy students a reassuringly limited audience and structured way to voice their ideas.

Whole-class interviews, on the other hand, can transform traditionally passive class activities—such as Show-and-Tell, Special Person of the Week, or student oral presentations—into interactive whole-class interviews in which the audience asks questions and responds to the speaker. This makes for a lively learning experience that reinforces the message that students can learn from each other. Likewise, whole-class interviews of guest speakers encourage students' sense of ownership of and responsibility for their own learning.

Getting Students Ready

Academic Preparation

Depending upon the interview purpose and your students' experience, use one or more of the preparation activities below to engage students' interest and hone their interviewing skills.

Introduce the topic. Tell a relevant personal story, read aloud a book, show and discuss an object, or in some other way connect students with the interview topic. If students will be asked specific information in their interviews—for example, to tell a family story or describe a favorite work of art—give students time to gather their data (or collect their thoughts) before the interview.

Invite an interviewer. Ask someone whose job involves interviewing—such as a journalist, social worker, or doctor—to speak to your students about the skills, process, and rewards of doing interviews in his or her profession. Or, an alternative would be to play a videotape of a familiar interviewer, such as Mr. Rogers, and discuss with students what they observe about his approaches and results.

Discuss questioning strategies. Teach effective questioning strategies by sharing the reasons behind how you ask questions. For example, discuss the difference between closed questions, which only elicit "yes" or "no" answers, and open questions that evoke more informative responses.

Model the process. Interview, and be interviewed by, a student or adult partner. (This not only gives students a chance to learn about the roles of interviewer and interviewee, but also to enjoy learning more about you when you are interviewed!) Afterwards, ask students to share their observations about the interviews—what worked, what didn't, what questions seemed most interesting or evocative, what questions they might have asked, and so on.

≈ HINT ≈

Different recording and reporting strategies can accommodate students' varying skill levels—for example, options include drawing a picture with a caption to show to the class, or taking brief notes to report to the class, or writing an expository paragraph or story to read aloud, and so on.

Social/Ethical Preparation

The following are some social and ethical aspects of interviewing that you may want to help your students anticipate.

Listening carefully. Listening well takes effort and practice. Encourage students to take their role as listeners as thoughtfully as they do other learning tasks—by clearing their desks and giving their full attention to the speaker. Ask students for their ideas on what behaviors might make a speaker feel listened to, and what might give the appearance of inattentiveness. For that matter, what can a speaker do to make it easier for a partner to listen?

Responding respectfully. Help students think about what kinds of responses help people feel "safe" expressing their thoughts and feelings. For example, how might they respond if their interviewee says something that doesn't make sense to them? That surprises them? That they disagree with? Students may enjoy role-playing the difference between respectful and disrespectful responses.

Being reported. When students report their partner's story or information, it can be very difficult for the partner to refrain from chiming in to add overlooked details or to correct the interviewer's rendition of their conversation. Ask students to think about how they feel when they are interrupted and why it is important to respect a partner's efforts to report an interview. Invite their suggestions for making the reporting process easier for everyone—for example, interviewers should check details with their partners before reporting, and after a report you could check in with the interviewee to see if he or she has anything to add, and so on.

Sharing the floor. For whole-class interviews, discuss with your students how they can share the interviewer role. For partner interviews, at first you will probably need to signal when it is time for partners to switch interviewer/interviewee roles; then as your students get the feel for doing interviews, ask for their ideas on how they can assume responsibility for dividing their interview time with their partner.

≈ HINT ≈

Get students in the habit of checking with their partner about what information is okay to share with the rest of the class—sometimes the partner might feel uncomfortable having something broadcast to the whole class.

WAYS TO USE *Interviewing*

ACTIVITIES   PARTNER INTERVIEWS

We Are Alike, We Are Different. Interviews about how partners are alike and different can help students appreciate their shared and unique traits—that it's fun to have things in common and interesting to be different. The activity can focus on specific subjects, such as what we like to learn, things we like to do with friends, areas of interest in a study topic, ways we like to get to know people, and so on. Introduce the activity with a whole-class brainstorm about what questions would be interesting and appropriate to ask in the interview. Have younger partners record their information in a three-column collage of magazine pictures or their own drawings—one column each for their unique traits or preferences, and the middle column for how they are alike; older students can demonstrate more sophisticated comparisons with a Venn diagram.

Talking Artifacts. This activity—in which partners bring in special objects from home, interview each other about them, and share what they have learned with the rest of the class—is another excellent vehicle for helping students get to know each other and build community in the classroom. (It works especially well with young children, as the use of tangible objects helps elicit and focus both their questions and responses.) Encourage students to bring in objects of personal rather than monetary value—for example, a letter from a grandparent, a favorite drawing, a photo of a friend or relative, and so on. Also, have them bring their object in a paper bag and keep it hidden until they are interviewed; this deters children from distracting each other with the fun of their artifacts and adds to the fun by heightening "suspense." Introduce the activity by bringing in an object of your own and having the class interview you about it. A useful variation on this interview would be to have students bring in (or bring in a picture of) a particular category of object, such as a favorite book, recording, work of art, or animal..

Someone Like . . . . To extend students' thinking about a story the class is reading, have partners interview each other about someone who reminds them of a character in the story—for example, an elderly person with whom they had a special relationship, like *Miss Maggie,* or a special pet like *Rosalie,* and so on. You could also use this interview before students have read the story, to introduce it and help them make personal connections with the ideas they will encounter in it.

Personal History. Partner interviews about family histories and traditions can enrich and humanize social studies and history lessons—for example, beginning a unit on state history by having partners interview each other about how their families came to the state. Introduce the activity several days before the interviews (perhaps by telling about your own history), so that students have time to gather information from parents or other family members.

Home Interviews. Have students use their interviewing skills outside of school, to interview a parent or other adult about something the class is studying. Before the interviews, have the class agree on three or four questions to use in the home interviews (these should be questions about opinions or universal experiences, not questions that require special knowledge or expertise). Afterwards, follow up with a class discussion or activity that allows students to share and benefit from what their classmates learned; similarly, students could share in partner interviews what they learned in their home interviews.

WHOLE-CLASS INTERVIEWS

Student Presentations. Have the class play the role of interviewer during current event reports, book reports, or other such presentations. Encourage the interviewers to probe beyond data and ask for the presenter's interpretation and speculations about his or her topic. An interesting variation would be for presenters to assume the identity of a character from the story or event being reported on and answer classmates' questions from the character's perspective.

Special Person of the Week. Students can take an enjoyable, active role in learning about the Special Person of the Week by conducting whole-class interviews. Ask the Special Person to share some special objects or photos with the class as a springboard for the interview, and model questioning strategies by participating in the interview yourself.

Guest Speakers. Guest speakers can help students learn about their school, community, and world, and students can take charge of their learning by interviewing the guest. Prior to the guest's visit, have students discuss what they would like to learn from the visitor and prepare interview questions accordingly. Guest speakers might include the following:

- members of students' families
- a substitute teacher (to give students insight into a substitute's experience!)
- school staff, such as the custodian, secretary, nurse, principal, or cafeteria worker
- representatives of different occupations, both familiar and unusual
- world travelers
- experts about something the class is studying

EXTENSIONS Interviewing activities can be extended in any of the following ways.

What Did We Learn? Invite students' comments about their experience of interviewing. What worked well? What might they do differently next time? What do they enjoy about doing interviews? How could they enjoy them more?

Make a Class Book. Have students each create a page (about their partner or about a whole-class interview, whichever the case may be) for a class book on the interview theme. The pages could also be displayed on a bulletin board.

Graphically Organize. After a partner interview, have students contribute what they learned to a class chart, Venn diagram, mural, or other graphic organization of information. For example, have students graph the number of siblings their partner has, fill in their partner's name on a Venn diagram about pets (who has a cat, dog, reptile, bird, etc.), mark a map showing the places their partner has visited or would like to visit, paint a picture of their partner's home on a map of the community, and so on. (See the Organizing Ideas formats on pages xx-xx for suggestions.)

Dramatize the Interview. Invite volunteers to dramatize their partner's experience or ideas, either solo or with the partner.

Poetry

POETRY accounts for some of the best-loved and most evocative literature in the world's cultures, yet people are often intimidated by it, as well. Fortunately, since most children begin enjoying poetry quite young (think of Dr. Seuss or Mother Goose), ignorant of any "accessibility" issues, the regular reading and writing of poetry in elementary school can lead to a lifelong comfort with and appreciation of the genre.

In fact, writing poetry appeals to many students, even those who otherwise do not enjoy writing, because it allows them to break conventions (for example, poets don't have to write in complete sentences) and because it stresses distilling ideas by using few rather than many words. And writing poetry with a group demonstrates the genre's flexibility even further: each group member contributes a line or section of the poem, and the whole group makes decisions about line order and form. As group members discuss their contributions, arrange and rearrange the lines, and help each other with language use and mechanics, they experience poetry (and language in general) as a powerful, malleable tool of communication.

WHY TO USE

- to help students appreciate and enjoy poetry
- to demystify poetry
- to encourage appreciation for different ways of seeing and saying things
- to give students a flexible, creative mode of self-expression

WHEN TO USE

- in response to an evocative issue, topic, story, or event
- as a follow-up to reading poetry that speaks to students
- when students have the skill to respond respectfully to one another's work

HOW TO DO

The Poetry format asks students to

- brainstorm and/or discuss ideas for the poem
- write their part of the poem
- read aloud their part of the poem to the rest of the group
- suggest, discuss, and agree on revisions to each other's writing
- with the group, decide on how to arrange the parts of the poem

Developmental Considerations

*Younger
students*

Jay birds land on wires very quickly.
I see lands of trees ahead of me
  when I look.

  *—A five-year-old's composition after looking through a
  pair of binoculars*

Young children have a knack for seeing and describing their world in unusual ways—ways that often move the rest of us to see things with new eyes. This ability to tweak our assumptions and help us look at the world differently makes young children natural poets, since this quality is also a hallmark of poetry.

Simply give children an engaging, immediate subject to write about; whereas older students can respond to more abstract topics, such as social issues or other people's experiences, younger children will do better with things they can see, touch, or personally relate to. For example, provide them with interesting experiences—observing an insect or animal, examining a rock or shell, gazing at the stars, or looking at the ordinary through a different lens, such as binoculars or a microscope—as the basis for writing poetry. Or tap into their feelings about important aspects of their lives—hopes, wishes, relationships with pets and people, and so on.

As for the actual writing of a group poem, emphasize ideas over form with young children—their group poems can simply be a mosaic of individual responses with minimal editing of each other's work. Encourage them to ask each other for help while working on their lines, but emphasize that the focus of cooperative poetry writing is expressing their thoughts, not the mechanics of writing. To that end, free verse poetry is ideal for young writers: lines can be of any length, they can be repeated, "sentences" can be incomplete, and syntax can be unconventional. Also to that end, beginning writers might write or dictate their lines, and students should feel free to use temporary spelling and punctuation on their first drafts.

I'll climb the highest tree and bring you back
  an apple.
I'll go on the biggest stage and I will sing
  the song you love.
I'll fly in the sky and bring you back the
  shiniest star.
If you want, I'll read a book for you.

  *—second-graders respond to the
  spirit of the book* Chicken Sunday

*Older
students*

Ziggy

Ziggy feels like a velvet teddy bear,

He looks like pancakes with syrup,

He smells like nature,

He sounds like he's interested,

Ziggy tastes like a steak fresh off
  the grill.

*—fifth-graders describe their
class rabbit*

≈HINT≈

*Because poetry is about
feelings, you'll always want
students to write about
topics they genuinely care
about. However, if a topic is
likely to be intensely personal, it is probably best
left for individual writing
rather than a group effort.*

Older students are more thoughtful about language and can experiment with different approaches to writing poetry, looking for the best
way to convey their ideas. Encourage this exploration—unfettered by
prose conventions, they may come up with some unique imagery (and
as a reader, allow yourself to be unfettered, too, and enjoy their cre-
·ations!). Likewise, as students work together, encourage their experi-
mentation by suggesting that they strive for interesting relationships
between ideas or sounds when putting together the individual parts of
their group poems.

Grouping Considerations

Once you have introduced the class to cooperative poetry by doing
some whole-class poems, you will probably find that small groups are
the best configuration for poetry activities—enough mix and variety of
ideas to keep things interesting, but not so many as to make the task
unwieldy. There are projects, of course, for which partner poems are
suitable.

Getting Students Ready

*Academic
Preparation*

The best preparation for writing poetry is being exposed to a variety of
good poetry—hearing it, reading it, and reading about it. Use the suggestions below to introduce your students to the many sounds of, and
ideas about, poetry.

Read Poetry. Read a variety of good poetry with the class—not just to
introduce cooperative poetry activities, but all the time and throughout
the curriculum. (Ways to Use Poetry, below, includes some suggested
sources of poetry and related activities.)

Read about Poetry. Sometimes hearing *about* poetry can inspire (and
reassure) students. The introduction and appendix to *Talking to the
Sun: An Illustrated Anthology of Poems for Young People* offer wonder-
fully practical and inspiring comments about poetry—for example:

"Different poems mean different things to different people at different times, but that isn't something you need to think about when you read a poem. In fact, worrying about finding the 'right' meaning can get in the way of your liking and understanding poetry. Just as you don't have to understand everything about your friends in order to enjoy them and learn things from them, so you don't have to understand everything about a poem to like it and get something from it." (This anthology, edited by Kenneth Koch and Kate Farrell and illustrated with works from New York's Metropolitan Museum of Art, is also a good source of poetry to read *to* students.)

Talk about Poetry. Introduce poetry activities by reading an adult poem and talking with students about a significant idea in the poem— an idea that will inspire their own poems. For example, in his book about teaching poetry to children (listed in Ways to Use Poetry, below), Kenneth Koch describes how after reading William Blake's "The Tyger" he has his students write a poem "in which you are talking to a beautiful and mysterious creature and you can ask it anything you want—anything. You have the power to do this because you can speak its secret language." Koch points out that "what matters for the present is not that the children admire Blake and his achievement, but that each child be able to find a tyger of his own."

Read and Talk about Poetry with a Poet. Invite a poet to the class to read his or her work and talk with students about writing poetry. (Many schools participate in Poets in the Schools programs, which can help you find a guest poet; get information about such programs from your principal or local or state arts council.)

Model the Process. Do some whole-class poetry writing to give students a foundation for their small-group work. Choose a topic, such as "Surprise is..." (or "Red is...," "Friendship is...," etc.), and write it on the board. Ask students to think about a time when they were surprised and how they could describe that experience in a phrase that begins "Surprise is...." Encourage them to think of many kinds of surprises. happy, silly, scary, and so on. Record students' responses on strips of paper, and with students' help arrange the strips into a poem. If students' descriptions lack detail, ask questions to help enliven their images; model ways to respectfully ask for clarification, make suggestions, and incorporate different people's ideas into one poem.

≈HINT≈

Use a pocket chart and sentence strips to make it easier for students to play with different line arrangements during whole-class and small-group poetry writing activities.

Social/Ethical Preparation

When creating a poem from their individual contributions, group members must be able to cooperate on several levels—in making and accepting constructive suggestions about each other's work, and in agreeing on the final composition of the poem. The following are some social and ethical aspects of poetry activities you may want to help students anticipate.

Responding respectfully. Help students appreciate that poets enable people to see things in new ways by saying things in new ways—and that perhaps they'll learn from each other's new way of saying things, too. Encourage them to think about how they could respond to a group

In Character. Adapt the activity above to help students gain insight into stories the class is reading. Choose a feeling that is a central element of a story (for example, Jimmy Jo's shyness in Katherine Paterson's *Come Sing, Jimmy Jo*), or have group members themselves identify a feeling theme. Ask students to put themselves in the character's place and write their feelings poem from the character's perspective.

Use Your Senses! In this activity, students work in small groups to explore how all the senses apply to an object, place, event, or concept—which can add thought-provoking dimensions to science, history, literature, and other curriculum areas. Have students observe and handle an interesting object and, focusing on one sense at a time, ask themselves such questions about the object as: If this had a taste, what might it taste like? What does the sound of this remind me of? What smells do I associate with this? What words would I use to describe what I see and feel? Encourage students to search for associations that linger just beyond literal descriptions. Each group member then composes a descriptive line based on one of the senses, and the group agrees on how to arrange the lines to create the poem. After students have experience writing about tangible objects, invite them to apply the senses to more abstract ideas (such as *friendship*, *guilt*, *green*, *success),* historical incidents, and so on.

≈ HINT ≈

Reading different line arrangements aloud may help groups decide on line order.

Art Poetry. Students are often asked to illustrate stories or poems— but the process is reversed for this activity, in which students write a poem inspired by a piece of art. Have small groups select an art print or photograph and create a poem about the picture; if possible, have available a wide variety of art for students to choose from (better yet, visit your local art museum and have students work from the real thing). To introduce the activity, show students an example of poetry translated to art in *Talking to the Sun:* on page 90, William Carlos Williams's "The Great Figure" is accompanied by a Charles Demuth painting inspired by the poem.

Story Poetry. As a variation on "Art Poetry," have partners or small groups use a favorite illustration or scene in a book as the basis for a poem about the story. For example, have each group member take a different character's perspective to write a line or verse about an illustration or passage. Or do a variation of Use Your Senses! and have group members write about a different sense—what a person or animal in the illustration might be seeing, hearing, tasting, smelling, and feeling.

EXTENSIONS   **What Did We Learn?** Give students a chance to talk about the group writing process. Based on your observations of group interactions, ask about a topic (or topics) most likely to yield an interesting discussion, for example: How did group members show consideration and respect for different ways of seeing or saying things? What kinds of suggestions did groupmates make about each other's work that proved helpful? Did any group have difficulty making decisions about line order? How did groups resolve such difficulties? What did students like about writing poetry with a group? What didn't they like? What might they do differently next time?

Poetry Reading. Have a poetry reading so that groups can share their work with each other. Give students time to plan and practice their presentations (for example, groups might choose a single reader or perform a choral reading), and discuss with the whole class the atmosphere they would like to create for the reading (do they want to present from a stage? serve refreshments? invite guests? have the option of playing recorded music to accompany their readings? and so on). If students seem inclined toward ambitious ideas for this event, hold a class meeting to discuss plans and assign responsibilities.

Poetry Art. Have groups illustrate their own or another group's poem, and compile a class book or bulletin board of these poetry–art partnerships.

Annotated Bibliography of Additional Resources

Laura E. Berk and Adam Winsler, *Scaffolding Children's Learning: Vygotsky and Early Childhood Education* **(National Association for the Education of Young Children, 1995).**

> As its title suggests, this book is focused on early childhood education and based on the theoretical perspective of Lev Vygotsky. Vygotsky's theory is very clearly presented and its implications for classroom practice are clearly drawn. The book applies Vygotsky's theory and related research to a variety of important issues and pedagogical approaches, such as working with children with serious learning and behavior problems, assessment, mixed-age grouping, reciprocal teaching, cooperative learning, and thematic instruction. While this book does not focus on moral development, it does a very good job of explicating how teachers might scaffold children's social interactions and social problem solving to help children reap the cognitive benefits of social interactions.
>
> Because we believe strongly that as teachers we should be striving for a coherent and comprehensive theory to guide our teaching, we want to comment on why we recommend books which are strongly based in two different theories—those of Vygotsky and Piaget. There are important similarities between them: in each theory, for example, the child is biologically programmed to develop knowledge of the world, and in each theory the development of knowledge involves active construction of meaning or understanding. Vygotsky places more stress than Piaget on the effects of the child's sociocultural context, and on the role of the adult or more competent other in aiding or scaffolding the child's development. But the two theories are not contradictory; they often imply similar pedagogical approaches, although different aspects of the learning process might be stressed in each. An important goal for educators in the future is to find ways to bring these two theories into complete alignment.

Carol Copple, Irving E. Sigel, and Ruth Saunders, *Educating the Young Thinker: Classroom Strategies for Cognitive Growth* **(D. Van Nostrand Company, 1979).**

> Based on Piaget's theory of cognitive development and Sigel's research in the development of children's ability to build symbolic representations of their world (representational competence), this book describes a coherent theory of education and a wide variety of practical activities and approaches for bringing the theory to life. Although the actual program described is a preschool program, the principles behind the activities are fully applicable to elementary classrooms. The focus is on teaching for understanding and on helping children build their representational competence by engaging them "in a variety of representational experiences, using inquiry systematically and carefully to encourage the children to 'distance' themselves from the here-and-now in time and space."
>
> The many anecdotes, teacher reflections, and concrete activities both clarify the theoretical perspective and provide concrete ideas for how to adapt the theory to a variety of settings.

Joan Dalton, *Adventures in Thinking: Creative Thinking and Co-operative Talk in Small Groups* **(Thomas Nelson Australia, 1990 edition).**

> In this book Joan Dalton describes practical guidelines for helping children work productively in cooperative groups and for developing their creativity and ability to communicate with others. The book also includes scores of practical activity units organized around engaging themes such as space, heroes, disasters, and the sea. For each unit there are numerous ideas for integrating all the language arts, suggestions for open-ended learning activities involving real learning purposes, and suggestions for different teaching strategies and groupings.

Joan Dalton and Julie Boyd, *I Teach: A Guide to Inspiring Classroom Leadership* **(Heinemann Educational Books, Inc., 1992).**

> "Classroom leaders: Provide real think-time . . . Trust their intuition . . . Listen more and talk less . . . Make explicit what is valued . . . Constantly seek to improve their learning and teaching . . ." These are examples of the more than one hundred principles of powerful teaching illustrated in this book. Working on the premise that powerful teachers possess "an enduring set of principles by which they teach and lead," Joan Dalton and Julie Boyd provide vivid and varied concrete examples of these principles in action in real classrooms. They group the principles under five goals of teaching: empowering others, exercising leadership, building relationships with others, creating a community of learners, and working on self-growth. When teachers are aware of these inner principles, they can use them as guidelines against which to measure external resources and demands, as guidelines for sound professional judgment.

Rheta DeVries and Betty Zan, *Moral Classrooms, Moral Children: Creating a Constructivist Atmosphere in Early Education* **(Teachers College Press, 1994).**

> Like the book by Copple, Sigel, and Saunders, this book is also based on the theory of Piaget and explicitly describes how that theory plays out in a preschool setting. DeVries and Zan, however, focus on a different goal—children's social and moral development—and on a different aspect of Piagetian theory—the role of the sociomoral atmosphere. Working from the same premise that the Child Development Project is based on, that children must construct their understanding of the social and moral world just as they do of the object world, this book examines different approaches to fostering children's sociomoral understanding. In addition to being well grounded in theory and research, this book provides detailed guidelines, examples, and anecdotes that clarify how to apply Piagetian/constructivist theory in a wide variety of common school situations—for example, conflict situations, group time, rule making, and discipline. Again like the Copple, Sigel, and Saunders book, its principles apply well beyond the preschool.

Harvard Education Letter, "Motivation, Achievement, and Testing," Edward Miller and Roberta Tovey, eds., *Harvard Education Letter,* **Focus Series No. 2 (1996).**

> This brief (24 pages) volume brings together ten articles from recent issues of HEL that discuss the issues and summarize recent findings from research related to academic motivation and achievement. The articles raise and clarify several issues affecting student motivation and achievement—for example, teachers' use of competition, rewards, and praise; stu-

dents' beliefs about the nature of intelligence and their ability to read teachers' expectations; and the role of testing and high standards. Each piece would make a good starting point for discussion by school staffs about how these issues apply in their classrooms and school.

Howard Gardner, *The Unschooled Mind: How Children Think and How Schools Should Teach* (Basic Books, 1991).

This scholarly and groundbreaking book traces the history of our beliefs about the nature and causes of human learning, makes a strong case for a biological/cultural approach to understanding human learning, and draws out the implications of this approach for, as the title says, how schools should teach. In this book, Gardner develops the concept of *teaching for understanding* and argues convincingly that this must be at least one of our major teaching goals. From this perspective, he discusses the strengths and weakness of several approaches to education, from those that focus on basic skills and cultural literacy to progressive education, and he describes several promising approaches for promoting student understanding. While critical of progressive education, Gardner does not reject it; rather, he sees it as the most promising base upon which to build new educational environments "in which genuine understanding can become a reality."

Alfie Kohn, *Beyond Discipline: From Compliance to Community* (Association for Supervision and Curriculum Development, 1996).

While a number of educators have abandoned the behaviorist approach to learning, few have done so for discipline or classroom management. Alfie Kohn argues that many of the most popular approaches to classroom management are firmly rooted in the behaviorist dictum that behavior is motivated by self-interest. Arguing for a more positive view of human nature based on current motivational and developmental theory and research, Kohn proposes that we take a less controlling and a more collaborative stance in our work with children.

Following a powerful and stinging critique of Assertive Discipline, the most popular of the behaviorist approaches, Kohn goes on to show that "more moderate" approaches, which he calls "punishment lite," are based in the same assumptions and are subject to the same criticisms. The problem, he points out, is that their goal is to control children, to gain compliance through manipulation. Instead, by changing our goal to that of working *with* children to develop their social and moral understanding and to build a caring classroom community, we can move beyond discipline to cooperative problem solving. Kohn offers numerous concrete suggestions for reaching this goal.

Catherine C. Lewis, *Educating Hearts and Minds: Reflections on Japanese Preschool and Elementary Education* (Cambridge University Press, 1995).

After all the stories we have heard about the rigidity of Japanese education and the academic superiority of Japanese students, we might expect Japanese elementary schools to be quiet places where teachers control their students and focus long hours on academic instruction. Catherine Lewis presents a surprisingly different picture. Through the voices of Japanese teachers and vivid examples from Japanese classrooms, Lewis helps us see teachers who focus on the development of the whole child—helping children build caring and responsible attitudes as well as helping them develop their understanding of academic content. In these classrooms children have time (sometimes a very long time) to struggle to understand academic content, they take responsibility for themselves and others, and they work and play cooperatively, enthusiastically, and happily. How do Japanese teachers accomplish all this?

As the chapters unfold we see an approach to education that is very consistent with the Deweyan principles of progressive education, with Piaget's theory of cognitive development and constructivist learning, and with the approach being advocated and described in *Among Friends*. While scholarly and well grounded in theory and research, this is not an academic book. It is truly a book for teachers, rich with provocative and instructive examples and at the same time respectful of American educational traditions.

Barbara L. McCombs and James E. Pope, *Motivating Hard to Reach Students* **(American Psychological Association, 1994).**

This book is designed to explain modern motivational theory, based (in contrast to behaviorist theory) on the recognition that individuals have a natural tendency to be intrinsically motivated to learn. It discusses the relevance of this theory to teaching, describes numerous strategies for helping individual students draw on their natural motivation to learn, and provides strategies for establishing a classroom climate that is likely to foster and sustain intrinsic motivation. The authors work through, and invite the reader to work through, numerous concrete situations applying motivational theory to help students better understand and value themselves and the learning process. The book contains helpful suggestions for applying these principles in the classroom—for example, suggestions for involving students in goal setting and in designing learning projects, and suggestions for encouraging academic risk-taking. Because it is a study guide, containing reflection questions and self-directed activities for the reader, this book might be especially helpful if worked through with a partner or group of fellow teachers.

John G. Nicholls, *The Competitive Ethos and Democratic Education* **(Harvard University Press, 1989).**

Tracing the development of children's understanding of the concepts of luck, effort, and ability, John Nicholls explains why children gradually move from unselfconscious involvement in tasks for pleasure or accomplishment to a self-conscious concern with doing better than others. He argues that common educational practices designed to motivate students, for example, public grading and extrinsic rewards for best performance, increase this tendency in children. When this self-conscious concern with doing better than others increases in prominence, Nicholls maintains that many students, generally those who fear that they will not do better than others, withdraw from learning opportunities, which results in their diminished accomplishment and their alienation from school.

How do we prevent this alienation? Reviewing the research on progressive learning environments—environments where children typically have choices in their learning activities and where they are helped to focus on the learning goals of the tasks—Nicholls argues that such environments lessen students' tendency to focus on doing better than others and provide all children with increased opportunities for learning. But the advantages of such learning environments do not stop with increased learning opportunities. Drawing from a series of studies with elementary and high school students, Nicholls reports that when children are helped to focus on learning instead of winning, they develop beliefs in the importance of working hard, working cooperatively, being interested in learning, and trying to understand instead of just memorize material. Further, when children are more focused on learning than winning, they are more likely to see the purpose of school as preparing them for useful work than as a means to achieve wealth and status.

While this is a somewhat technical book, it is written in a clear style with lots of practical examples of ways teachers can increase the task involvement of their students.

Nel Noddings, *The Challenge to Care in Schools: An Alternative Approach to Education* (Teachers College Press, 1992).

Arguing not from psychological or developmental theory and research, but from the premise that "To care and be cared for are fundamental human needs," Nel Noddings outlines an approach to schooling which is both similar to and different from the approaches described in the above books and to the approach advocated by the Child Development Project. She describes the ways in which our schools have become uncaring places, pointing to increased school size, a focus on behavioral objectives and standardized teaching methods, and the rise of accountability and a pervasive need to control teachers, students, and content. She argues that the central goal of schooling "should be to promote the growth of students as healthy, competent, moral people."

Noddings carefully analyzes what it means to be moral and to care, and makes many recommendations for school change. For example, in the chapter on "Caring and Continuity," she argues that for schools to be caring environments for children they must be places where children experience stability of place and of personal relationships—enough stability to satisfy children's strong need for a sense of belonging. Some of her recommendations require only modest changes, such as keeping children with the same class and teacher two or more years, and some require major changes, such as totally revamping the curriculum around themes of care. Whether modest or major, each recommendation is carefully supported and likely to provoke new ways of looking at schools and spark new ideas for making them more caring places.

Bob Strachota, *On Their Side: Helping Children Take Charge of Their Learning* (Northeast Foundation for Children, 1996).

In this very personal and practical book, Bob Strachota, an elementary school teacher for twenty-five years, tells about his teaching experiences after he changed his teaching approach from telling children what they should know or what they should do to "wondering with" children. He tells us he began by clarifying his goals and outlining three basic principles to guide his teaching. "My goal is to help children take responsibility for inventing their own understanding of how the world works and of how to live ethically. To achieve my goal I center my teaching around three practices: *I ally with the children . . . I ask real questions . . . I share responsibility . . .*" He then goes on to show in a wide variety of classroom and school situations how these principles help him create a classroom with high learning and ethical standards where children bear substantial responsibility for both.

The many anecdotes and personal reflections he shares help us see how he achieves his goal, how he struggles with difficult situations, and how he manages both to accept children where they are and hold high expectations for their learning and development.

Teacher Index

CLASSROOM SPOTLIGHT

KINDERGARTEN

GRADE 1

GRADE 2–3

GRADE 3

GRADE 4

GRADE 4–5

GRADE 5–6

GRADE 6

COLLEAGUES CONVERSE

INTERVIEWS

KINDERGARTEN

GRADE 1

Teacher Support Materials from Developmental Studies Center

Among Friends: Classrooms Where Caring and Learning Prevail
In classroom vignettes and conversations with teachers across the country, this 208-page book provides concrete ideas for building caring learning communities in elementary school classrooms. With a focus on how the ideas of the research-based Child Development Project (CDP) play out in practice, Australian educator Joan Dalton and CDP Program Director Marilyn Watson take us into classrooms where teachers make explicit how they promote children's intellectual, social, and ethical development simultaneously throughout the day and across the curriculum. A chapter on theory and research provides a coherent rationale for the approach teachers demonstrate.

At Home in Our Schools
The 136-page book focuses on schoolwide activities that help educators and parents create caring school communities. It includes ideas about leadership, step-by-step guidelines for 15 activities, and reproducible planning resources and suggestions for teachers. The 12-minute overview video is designed for use in staff meetings and PTO/parent gatherings to create support for a program of whole-school activities. The 48-page study guide structures a series of organizing meetings for teachers, parents, and administrators.

The Collegial Study Package includes the book, the overview video, and the study guide.

Blueprints for a Collaborative Classroom
This "how-to" collection of partner and small-group activities is organized into 25 categories that cover the waterfront—from a quick partner interview to a complex research project. Over 200 activity suggestions are included for all elementary grades, in categories like Mindmapping, Decision-Making, Partner Reading, Editing, and Investigating. In addition, Fly-on-the-Wall vignettes offer insights from real classrooms. (176 pages)

Choosing Community: Classroom Strategies for Learning and Caring
In nine videotaped presentations, author and lecturer Alfie Kohn describes pivotal choices that promote community and avoid coercion and competition in classrooms. A 64-page facilitator's guide for use in staff development accompanies the presentations, which include such topics as "The Case Against Competition," "The Consequences of 'Consequences,'" "The Trouble with Rewards," and "Beyond Praise and Grades." The package also includes Kohn's influential book *Punished by Rewards: The Trouble with Gold Stars, Incentive Plans, A's, Praise and Other Bribes.*

Homeside Activities (K–5)
Six separate collections of activities by grade level help teachers, parents, and children communicate. Each 128-page collection has an introductory overview, 18 reproducible take-home activities in English and Spanish, and suggestions for teachers on integrating the activities into the life of the classroom. The 12-minute overview video is designed for use at parent gatherings and staff meetings as an overview of a program of Homeside Activities. The 48-page study guide structures a series of teacher meetings for collegial study inservice.

The Collegial Study Package includes one each K–5 books, the overview video, the study guide, and a 31-minute video documenting 3 classrooms and parents working at home with their children.

Number Power (Grades K–6)
Each 192-page teacher resource book offers three replacement units (8–12 lessons per unit) that foster students' mathematical and social development. Students collaboratively investigate problems, develop their number sense, enhance their mathematical reasoning and communication skills, and learn to work together effectively.

Reading, Thinking & Caring: Literature-Based Reading (Grades K–3)
A children's literature program to help students love to read, think deeply and critically, and care about how they treat themselves and others. Teaching units are available for over 80 classic, contemporary, and multicultual titles. Each 3- to 10-day unit includes a take-home activity in English and Spanish to involve parents in their children's life at school. Also available are grade-level sets and accompanying trade books.

Reading for Real: Literature-Based Reading (Grades 4–8)
A literature-based program to engage the student's conscience while providing interesting and important reading, writing, speaking, and listening experiences. Teaching units are available for over 100 classic, contemporary, and multi-cultural titles, and each 1- to 3-week unit includes a take-home activity to involve parents in children's life at school. Also available are grade-level sets and accompanying trade books.

Reading for Real Collegial Study
Videotaped classroom vignettes illustrate key concepts and common stumbling blocks in facilitating literature-based classroom discussion. A 64-page study guide structures a series of five collegial study meetings that cover the following topics: "Reflecting and Setting Goals," "Responding to Students," "Handling Offensive Comments and Sensitive Topics," "Guiding Students' Partner Discussions," and "Assessing Student Progress."

That's My Buddy! Friendship and Learning Across the Grades
The 140-page book is a practical guide for two buddy teachers or a whole staff. It draws on the experiences of teachers from DSC's Child Development Project schools across the country. The 12-minute overview video is designed for use at staff meetings to build interest in a schoolwide buddies program. The 48-page study guide structures a series of teacher meetings for collegial study and support once a buddies program is launched.

The Collegial Study Package includes the book, the overview video, and the study guide.

Ways We Want Our Class To Be: Class Meetings That Build Commitment to Kindness and Learning
The 116-page book describes how to use class meetings to build a caring classroom community and address the academic and social issues that arise in the daily life of the elementary school classroom. In addition to tips on getting started, ground rules, and facilitating the meetings, 14 guidelines for specific class meetings are included. The 20-minute overview video visits a variety of class meetings in grades K–5/6 and includes teacher interviews.The Class Meetings Package includes, in addition to the book and overview video, a 48-page study guide to help structure a series of teacher meetings for collegial study and video documentation of seven classrooms where students are involved in planning and decision making, checking in on learning and behavior, and problem solving.

The Collegial Study Package includes the book, the overview video, the study guide, and 99 minutes of video documenting 7 classrooms.